YOUR
Confirmation

A CHRISTIAN HANDBOOK FOR ADULTS

JOHN STOTT

With study guide by Lance Pierson

Sean Boland.

Hodder & Stoughton
LONDON   SYDNEY   AUCKLAND   TORONTO

British Library Cataloguing in Publication Data
ISBN 0 340 55700 1 (casebound)
ISBN 0 340 52180 5 (paperback)

Designed and created by Three's Company 12 Flitcroft Street London WC2H 8DJ.

Worldwide co-edition organised and produced by Angus Hudson Ltd, Concorde House, Grenville Place, Mill Hill, London NW7 3SA.

Published by Hodder and Stoughton, a division of Hodder and Stoughton Ltd, Mill Road, Dunton Green, Sevenoaks, Kent, TN13 2YA. Editorial Office: 47 Bedford Square, London WC1B 3DP.

Photoset by Watermark, Cromer. Printed in Singapore.

contents

Abbreviations

ASB   The Alternative Service Book 1980.
AV   The Authorized (King James') Version of the Bible (1611).
LXX   The Old Testament in Greek according to the Septuagint,
      3rd century BC.
NIV   The New International Version of the Bible
      (1973, 1978, 1984).
RSV   The Revised Standard Version of the Bible
      (NT 1946, 2nd Edition 1971; OT 1952).

Preface to the Second Edition

Your Confirmation was first published as part of the 'Christian Commitment Series' in 1958. During the third of a century which has elapsed since then, both the world and the church have changed. The world (at least in the west) has become more secular, more sceptical, more critical, while the churches have tried to face up to the challenges of modernity. One example of this, in the case of Anglican churches, has been the adoption of revised prayer books as alternatives to the Book of Common Prayer. This second edition of *Your Confirmation* seeks to reflect these changes. It is the same book, in the sense that it has the same outline, but it has been completely re-written.

I have tried to keep several kinds of people in mind.

To begin with, there are confirmation candidates themselves, who see their preparation period as a heaven-sent opportunity to think out what it means to be a Christian in today's world, and who want to get their teeth into something fairly solid. It is an interesting statistic that, although the number of people being confirmed in this country is declining, their average age is rising. About one third of them are now adults. So I have written mainly for them, though also for thoughtful students who are either at college or approaching the end of their school career.[1]

Then there are newly confirmed people, who want to explore further the implications of their recent confirmation, the privileges of full church membership, and the responsibilities of Christian belief and behaviour.[2]

In addition, there may be mature Christians, whose confirmation took place long ago, whose memory of their pre-confirmation instruction is decidedly rusty, and who feel the need of a refresher course in Christian fundamentals.

At whatever stage you are in your spiritual journey, I pray that something or other in this little book may help you to 'grow in the grace and knowledge of our Lord and Saviour Jesus Christ' (2 Peter 3:18). I thank the Rev. George Weld and the Rev. Andy Pavlibeyi for making suggestions for the revision of the first edition; Toby Howarth and Todd Shy for also reading the MS of the second edition and making valuable comments; Lance Pierson for preparing the Study Guide; David Porter for the suggestions on further reading; Carolyn Armitage, Tim Dowley and Peter Wyart for their help in designing the second edition of this book; and Frances Whitehead for yet another polished typescript.

John Stott
September 1990

---

[1] I warmly recommend two books for confirmation candidates in their middle teens. *To be Confirmed* ... by Gavin Reid (Hodder, 1977) uses 'a popular newspaper approach' and is easy to follow. *Towards Confirmation* by John Eddison (Marshalls, 1982) is simple to understand, being enlivened by anecdotes and other illustrations. For adults I recommend *I Want to be a Christian* by J. I. Packer (Tyndale House in USA and Kingsway in UK, 1977). Its author describes it as 'a resource-book for groups and also a do-it-yourself catechism course for adults who have no access to such a group.' It is in four parts, covering the Apostles' Creed, Baptism and Conversion, the Lord's Prayer and the Ten Commandments. It contains rich, biblical teaching.

[2] I recommend two books for the newly confirmed. *Believing and Belonging* by Richard Gorrie (Falcon, 1980) is intended for members of a church youth group. *Going On* (Daybreak, 1989) was written by Bishop John B. Taylor for people he confirms in the Diocese of St. Albans. It deserves a wider readership. He succeeds in his aim of being readable.

General hints on using the study guide

Basic

A simple outline for a short study, based entirely on the chapter it follows. It can be used by an individual reader, or by a group working together. It should take between 30 and 60 minutes, depending on how thoroughly you go into the questions, and how quickly you work.

Questions

Based on the chapter. Check your answer with what John Stott wrote; or if you are stuck, use his words to help you form your answer.

If you are working alone, write your answers down, perhaps in note form. If you are in a group, discuss together; pause to think on your own first, then compare your answers. It may help sometimes to do this in two's, three's or four's, rather than the full circle. When asked how you would answer or explain to someone, it may help to try the conversation out with someone who really feels that way, or can pretend to.

Promise

Taken from the list on p. 36. Learn one of these verses by heart to help you in times of doubt or temptation.

Prayer

Taken from the selection on pp. 157–160.

Say the chosen prayer as a way of responding to God on the theme of this chapter. By all means add other prayers of your own.

Extras

Some other approaches to studying the chapter's theme. You could add them to the items above, if you have time; or replace one of those with one of these.

Bible study

Here is a longer Bible passage giving further insight into the theme of this chapter. If there is not time to study it now, you could read it later before you go on to the next chapter.

In a group

If you are working on this book in a group, here is an idea to help you share ideas and experiences together. It may fit in well at the beginning of the session, or perhaps at the end.

Response

Here is a more varied way of responding to God, to go alongside the set prayers from pp. 157–160.

Check-up

A personal, challenging question summing up the main aim of the chapter. Lay it before God in a prayerful attitude, and try to answer it honestly. If your answer is No, or Not sure, who should you talk to or what action should you take?

Leaders of Confirmation or Basics courses may like to discuss this question in a personal conversation with each member.

Introduction:
What is Confirmation?

Your confirmation is obviously an event of great importance. Publicly – before your family, friends and a Christian congregation – you declare that you have committed your life to Jesus Christ and want to follow him. Then the bishop, by laying his hands on your head, assures you of God's acceptance, welcomes you into full membership of the church, and prays that you will be given grace to be faithful.

You may have been baptized as a baby. In that case, you were also signed 'with the cross, the sign of Christ' and exhorted to 'fight valiantly under the banner of Christ'. Your parents and godparents, in bringing you to baptism, affirmed 'their allegiance to Christ and their rejection of all that is evil'. They were also asked to express before God and the church their personal 'belief and trust in ... God the Father who made the world, ... in his Son Jesus Christ who redeemed mankind, ... and in his Holy Spirit who gives life to the people of God'. This declaration of faith and commitment they made on your behalf, undertaking to bring you up to believe in God, to fight evil and to follow Christ. Now, however, the question is whether you are ready to make this declaration in your own name, and personally to enlist as a soldier of Christ. For the bishop will say to you:

> You have come here to be confirmed. You stand in the presence of God and his Church. With your own mouth and from your own heart you must declare your allegiance to Christ and your rejection of all that is evil.

Alternatively, you may have come to faith in Christ as an adult, not having been baptized as a baby. In that case, you are preparing to be baptized and confirmed on the same day, and probably in the same service. For adult converts like yourself, your baptism is in itself a complete 'initiation' into Christ. By faith (inwardly) and baptism (outwardly) you become a full member of Christ and his

Many of those confirmed today are adults.

church. No further ceremony like confirmation is strictly necessary. It is true that the apostles Peter and John laid their hands on some Samaritans who had already been baptized (Acts 8:12–17), and that the apostle Paul laid his hands on some Ephesians who had been baptized (Acts 19:1–7). In these two situations also, it was at the time of the laying on of apostolic hands that the people concerned received the Holy Spirit. But it is clear from Luke's developing story of the spread of the gospel that these were special cases (Samaritans on the one hand and disciples of John the Baptist on the other). The apostles did not regularly lay their hands on baptized converts, nor was the Holy Spirit regularly given and received in that way. God's normal way was to give the Holy Spirit to all those who repented, believed and were baptized, without any laying on of hands (e.g. Acts 2:38).

The purpose of confirmation
We must therefore resist the idea (common but mistaken) that the purpose of confirmation by the bishop is to 'give' the Holy Spirit. No, people who come to confirmation are (or should be) already

Christian believers, who already belong to Christ and therefore have the Holy Spirit living in them (Romans 8:9). What then is the point of confirmation for those who are converted and baptized as adults? If confirmation is not necessary to complete their initiation, why retain it? I think the answer is that the laying on of hands is a biblical sign which occurred in a wide variety of situations. It was used, for example, in seeking God's blessing on the young (e.g. Genesis 48:14–16; Mark 10:16), in praying for the healing of the sick (e.g. Luke 4:40; Acts 9:17), in ordaining people to the pastoral ministry (e.g. 1 Timothy 4:14; 5:22; 2 Timothy 1:6), and in commissioning missionaries and other Christian workers (e.g. Acts 6:1–6; 13:1–3), in addition to the two special occasions in Samaria and Ephesus which I have just mentioned. Then, at least as early as the third century, the church included a laying on of hands in its baptism service. Because in itself it was a seemly biblical practice, the sixteenth century Reformers saw no reason to discontinue its use. They separated it from baptism, however, and retained it as a pastorally appropriate gesture to accompany admission to full church membership.

Perhaps, however, you belong to a third category. In your case you have already been both baptized and received into church membership of another Protestant church, but now wish to become an Anglican. There is of course no question of your being re-baptized. In many ways it should be sufficient for your vicar to welcome you into membership simply by giving you 'the right hand of fellowship' (Galatians 2:9). To insist on episcopal confirmation may seem an unnecessarily elaborate procedure. On the other hand, the bishop represents the wider Anglican church, so that the laying on of his hands symbolizes a welcome wider than to a purely local congregation.[1]

Two meanings

To whichever of these three groups you may belong, it is natural now to ask: why is this service called a 'confirmation'? The Book of Common Prayer and most additional Anglican prayer books use the word in two ways, namely to describe both what you do and what God does in the service. You 'confirm' your commitment to Christ, whether this means ratifying personally what was promised in your name at your baptism, or affirming publicly what has previously been private, or renewing in the present what you have said and done in the past. Then God 'confirms' you as, through the laying on of his hands, the bishop both prays for God's blessing on you and assures you of it.

To find a clear statement of these two meanings of 'confirmation', especially the first, one needs to go back to the 1662 Book of Common Prayer. In that book's confirmation service the bishop asks:

> Do ye here, in the presence of God and of this congregation, renew the solemn promise and vow that was made in your name in your baptism, ratifying and *confirming* the same in your own persons, and acknowledging yourselves bound to believe and to do all those things which your godfathers and godmothers then undertook for you?

Because in the Alternative Service Book (1980) and in other contemporary Anglican prayer books the reference to godparents is omitted, the reference to 'confirming' the promises made by them is naturally omitted also. Instead, those who are to be confirmed make their own public declaration of repentance, faith and commitment, irrespective of when their baptism has taken place.

They then kneel, and the bishop lays his hands on them, praying for each '*Confirm*, O Lord, your servant N with your Holy Spirit'. After the confirmation he adds the following petition, often inviting the people to join with him:

> Defend, O Lord, your servants with your heavenly grace, that they may continue yours for ever, and daily increase in your Holy Spirit more and more, until they come to your everlasting kingdom.

What, then, does the laying on of hands signify? The bishop explains his action in the prayer which follows. It begins,

> Heavenly Father, we pray for your servants upon whom we have now laid our hands, after the example of the apostles, to assure them by this sign of your favour towards them. May your fatherly hand ever be over them, your Holy Spirit ever be with them ... .

Confirmation is thus intended to give a public assurance of God's blessing, and the bishop's hand is regarded as a symbol of the fatherly hand of God who promises to hold and guide his children.

Here, then, is the double meaning of confirmation. It is an opportunity to confirm and to be confirmed. It is a chance publicly to declare yourself a Christian and equally publicly to be assured by the bishop's hand and voice that you are what you have said you are.

So what exactly is a Christian? Confirmation obliges us to ask and answer this question, which is what we will seek to do in the next chapter.

---

[1] In the case of Roman Catholics wishing to join the Church of England or one of its sister churches, the Anglican practice is to recognize their baptism and confirmation, and to 'receive' them into membership by requiring them to answer a few appropriate questions and by extending to them the right hand of fellowship.

Christian Beginnings

In seeking to define what a Christian is, it is necessary to draw a distinction between 'nominal' and 'committed' Christians. It may seem invidious, and it is certainly distasteful, to have to distinguish, but in doing so we are only following the biblical authors who lay much stress on the difference between outward profession and inward reality. It is possible to be a Christian in name without being a Christian in heart.

1. How to Become a Christian

What Christianity is not

So many and widespread are the misconceptions of Christianity today, that I need to tackle these first. It is often necessary to demolish before one can build. What then is the essence of Christianity?

First, Christianity is not primarily a *creed*. Many people think it is. They imagine that if they can recite the Apostles' Creed from beginning to end without any mental reservations, this will make them a Christian. In conversation with a consultant physician some years ago, I remember asking him what he thought a Christian was. After a few moments' thought he replied, 'A Christian is someone who assents to certain dogmas.' But his answer was inadequate to the point of inaccuracy. Of course Christianity has a creed, and Christian belief is very important, but it is possible to assent to all the articles of the Christian faith and not be a Christian. The best proof of that is the devil. As James wrote: 'You believe that there is one God. Good! Even the demons believe that – and shudder' (James 2:19).

Secondly, Christianity is not primarily a *code of conduct*. Yet many suppose that it is, and even contradict the people who belong to our first category. 'It really doesn't matter what you believe', they say, 'so long as you lead a decent life'. So they struggle to keep the Ten Commandments, to live up to the standards of the Sermon on the Mount, and to follow the Golden Rule. All of which is fine and noble, but the essence of Christianity is not ethics. To be sure, it has an ethic, indeed the highest ethic the world has ever known, with its supreme law of love. But it is possible to live an upright life and not be a Christian, as many agnostics can testify.

Thirdly, Christianity is not primarily a *cult*, using the word in the sense of 'a system of religious worship' and a cluster of ceremonies. Of course Christianity has certain observances. The gospel sacraments of Baptism and Holy Communion, for example, were instituted by Jesus himself and have been enjoyed by the church ever since. Both are precious and profitable. Further, this book is about confirmation, so that I shall not be thought to belittle that ordinance! Church membership and church attendance are necessary parts of the Christian life; so are prayer and Bible reading. But it is possible to engage in these outward practices and still miss the core of Christianity. The Old Testament prophets were constantly denouncing the Israelites for their empty religion, and Jesus criticized the Pharisees for the same thing.

So Christianity is neither a creed, nor a code, nor a cult, important as these are in their place. It is in essence neither an intellectual, nor an ethical nor a ceremonial system. Indeed, we must go further. It is not all three put together. It is perfectly possible (though rare because difficult) to be orthodox in belief, upright in conduct and conscientious in religious observances, and still to overlook the heart of Christianity.

Christianity is not primarily a cluster of ceremonies.

John Wesley's Holy Club

Perhaps the best historical example of this is John Wesley in his Oxford days before his conversion. He, his brother Charles and some of their mutual friends founded a religious society in 1729 which came to be known as 'the Holy Club'. Its members seem to have been admirable in every way. First, they were orthodox in their faith. They believed not only the Apostles' Creed, the Nicene Creed and Athanasius's Creed, but the Thirty-Nine Articles of the Church of England as well.

Secondly, they lived an impeccable life. Meeting together several evenings each week, they studied improving literature and tried to perfect their timetable, so that every minute of every day had its appointed duty. They then began to visit the prisoners in the Oxford Castle and the Bocardo (for debtors). Next they founded a school in a slum area, paying the teacher and clothing the children out of their own pockets. They were full of good works.

Thirdly, they were very religious. They attended Holy Communion every week, fasted on Wednesdays and Fridays, kept the canonical hours of prayer, observed Saturday as the sabbath as well as Sunday, and followed the austere discipline of Tertullian, the early Latin church father.

Yet in spite of this extraordinary combination of orthodoxy, philanthropy and piety, John Wesley later reckoned that he was not a Christian at all at the time. Writing to his mother he confessed that, although his faith may perhaps have been that of 'servants', it certainly was not the faith of 'sons'. Religion to him meant bondage, not freedom.

In 1735 he sailed for Georgia as a chaplain to the colonists and a missionary to the Indians. But two years later, deeply disillusioned, he returned. He wrote in his journal: 'I went to America to convert the Indians; but oh! who shall convert me?' Again, 'What have I learned myself in the mean time? Why, what I the least of all suspected, that I, who went to America to convert others, was never myself converted to God'.[1] We will return to Wesley later.

What Christianity is

What, then, was missing? If the essence of Christianity is neither a creed, nor a code, nor a cult, what is it? It is Christ! It is not primarily

John Wesley
(1703–1791),
the great English
evangelist.

THE WORLD IS MY PARISH.

a system of any kind; it is a person, and a personal relationship to that person. Then other things fit into place – our beliefs and behaviour, our church membership and church attendance, and our private and public devotions. But Christianity without Christ is a frame without a picture, a casket without a jewel, a body without breath. The apostle Paul put it succinctly in his letter to the Philippians. Having described Christians as those 'who glory in Christ Jesus and who put no confidence in the flesh (i.e. in themselves)', he went on:

But whatever was to my profit I now consider loss for the sake of Christ. What is more, I consider everything a loss compared to the surpassing greatness of knowing Christ Jesus my Lord, for whose sake I have lost all things. I consider them rubbish, that I may gain Christ and be found in him, not having a righteousness of my own that comes from the law, but that which is through faith in Christ – the righteousness that comes from God and is by faith. (Philippians 3:7–9).

We learn from this great, personal statement of Paul's that, first of all, to be a Christian is *to know Christ as our Friend*. Perhaps 'friend' sounds too familiar. But Jesus himself used the word when he said 'I have called you friends' (John 15:15). And all the New Testament authors tell of an intimate relationship with him. Peter says that 'though you have not seen him, you love him' (1 Peter 1:8). John writes that 'we are in him who is true, even in his Son Jesus Christ' (1 John 5:20). And Paul bears witness to 'the surpassing greatness of knowing Christ Jesus my Lord' (Philippians 3:8). He is not referring to an intellectual knowledge about Christ, but to a personal knowledge of Christ. We all know about Christ – his birth and boyhood, his trade, his words and works, his death and resurrection. The question is whether we can say with integrity that we know him, that he is the supreme reality in our lives.

Paul expressed it in a way which is likely to appeal to business people, for he drew up a kind of profit and loss account. He wrote down in one column everything which had previously seemed profitable to him – his ancestry, inheritance, upbringing, education, righteousness and religious zeal. In the other column he wrote simply 'the knowledge of Jesus Christ'. Then he made a careful calculation and concluded that in comparison with 'the overwhelming gain of knowing Christ Jesus my Lord' (J. B. Phillips), everything else was loss. That is to say, knowing Christ is an experience of such outstanding value that, compared with it, even the most precious things in our lives seem like rubbish. It is an amazing and challenging claim.

Gaining Christ

Secondly, to be a Christian is *to trust Christ as our Saviour*. Paul writes not only of 'knowing Christ' but of 'gaining him' and 'being found in him'. He then explains this in terms of an important contrast: 'not having a righteousness of my own that comes from the law (i.e. from obeying it), but that which ... comes from God by faith' in Christ. It sounds complicated, but can be unravelled without too much difficulty. It is all about 'righteousness'. What did Paul mean?

Since God is righteous, it stands to reason that if we are ever to enter his presence, we must be righteous too. But where can we hope to obtain a righteousness which will fit us for the presence of God? There are only two possible answers to that question. The first is that we will try to establish our own righteousness by our good deeds and religious observances. Many make this attempt. But it is doomed to failure, because in God's sight 'all our righteous acts are like filthy rags'(Isaiah 64:6). All those who have even glimpsed God's glory have been overwhelmed by the sight and by a sense of their own sinfulness. It is therefore impossible to make ourselves good enough for God. If we think we can, we must have either a very low view of God or a very exaggerated view of ourselves, or probably both.

Trusting Christ

The only alternative to our achieving a righteous standing before God is that we receive it as a free gift of God through putting our trust in Jesus Christ. For Jesus Christ himself lived a perfectly righteous life; he had no sins of his own for which atonement needed to be made. But on the cross he identified himself with our unrighteousness. He took our place, bore our sin, paid our penalty, died our death. Indeed, 'God made him who had no sin to be sin for us, so that in him we might become the righteousness of God' (2 Corinthians 5:21). If, therefore, we come to Christ and put our trust in him, a marvellous but mysterious exchange takes place. He takes away our sins, and clothes us with his righteousness instead. In consequence, we stand before God 'not trusting in our own righteousness, but in God's manifold and great mercies' (Book of Common Prayer), not in the tattered rags of our own morality but in the spotless robe of the righteousness of Christ. And God accepts us not because we are righteous, but because the righteous Christ died for our sins and was raised from death.

This is the truth which came home to John Wesley when on 24th May 1738 he visited a Moravian meeting in Aldersgate Street, East London. As somebody was reading Luther's preface to his commentary on the Letter to the Romans, in which Luther explained the meaning of 'justification by faith alone', a personal faith in Christ was born in Wesley's heart. He wrote in his Journal: 'I felt my heart strangely warmed. I felt I did trust in Christ, Christ alone for salvation; and an assurance was given me that he had taken away my sins, even mine, and saved me from the law of sin and death.'[2] The operative words are that he now trusted 'in Christ alone for salvation'. For years he had been trusting in himself (his orthodox belief, charitable works and religious zeal); but now at last he came to put his trust in Christ as his Saviour. We ourselves must do the same.

Thirdly, to be a Christian is *to obey Christ as our Lord.* For Paul wrote of knowing 'Christ Jesus my Lord'. The lordship of Jesus is a much neglected truth today. We continue to pay lip-service to it and often allude to Jesus politely as 'our Lord'. But he still asks, as he did in the Sermon on the Mount, 'Why do you call me "Lord, Lord", and do not do what I say?' (Luke 6:46). 'Jesus is Lord' was the earliest of all Christian confessions (see Romans 10:9; 1 Corinthians 12:3; Philippians 2:11), and it has enormous implications. For when Jesus is truly our Lord, he directs our lives and we gladly obey him. Indeed, we bring every part of our lives under his lordship – our home and family, our sexuality and marriage, our job or unemployment, our money and possessions, our ambitions and recreations.

Commitment to Christ

We have seen that, in essence, Christianity is Christ. It is a personal relationship to Christ as our Saviour, Lord and Friend. But how does one become committed to him in this way? Let me suggest that there are four steps for us to take, which (to help fasten them in memory) begin with the letters A, B, C and D.

Something to Admit

A stands for something to *Admit*. Our very first step is to admit that (to use the traditional vocabulary) we are 'sinners' and need a 'Saviour'. By 'sin' the Bible means self-centredness. God's order is that we love him first, our neighbour next and ourselves last. Sin is precisely the reversal of this order. It is to put ourselves first, our neighbour next (when it suits our convenience) and God somewhere in the distant background. Instead of loving God with all our being, we have rebelled against him and gone our own way. Instead of loving and serving our neighbours, we have selfishly fostered our own interests. In our better moments we know this and feel thoroughly ashamed.

Moreover, our sins separate us from God. For he is absolutely pure and holy. He can neither live with evil, nor look upon it, nor come to terms with it. The Bible speaks of him as being like a blinding light and a consuming fire. So his 'wrath' (which is not any kind of personal malice, but his righteous hostility to sin) rests upon us. In consequence, our greatest need is a 'Saviour' who can span the gulf which yawns between us and God, since the bridges we try to build do not reach the other side. We need God's forgiveness and a new start.

This first step is probably the hardest of the four to take, because we find it humiliating. We greatly prefer to build up our self-esteem and self-confidence, and insist that we can manage by ourselves. In that state of mind we shall never come to Christ. As he put it, 'it is not the healthy who need a doctor, but the sick. I have not come to call the righteous (i.e. the self-righteous), but sinners' (Mark 2:17). In other words, just as we do not go to the doctor unless we are ill and admit it, so we will not go to Christ unless we are sinners and admit it. The proud refusal to acknowledge this has kept more people out of the kingdom of God than anything else. We have to humble ourselves and admit that self-salvation is impossible.

Something to Believe

B stands for something to *Believe*, namely that Jesus Christ is the very Saviour we have just admitted we need. Indeed, he is uniquely qualified to save sinners because of who he is and what he has done.

Who is he? He is the eternal Son of God who became a human being in Jesus of Nazareth, and is the one and only God-man. What has he done? After a public ministry characterized by selfless service, he deliberately went to Jerusalem and to the cross. He had foretold that he would voluntarily 'lay down his life' for us (e.g. John 10:11, 18), and that he would 'give his life as a ransom' for us (Mark 10:45). By this he indicated both that we were prisoners unable to escape and that the price he would pay for our release was the sacrifice of his own life. He would die instead of us, in our place. Just as he had taken our human nature to himself at his birth, so he would take our sin and guilt to himself at his death. And this is what he did. On the cross he endured in his innocent person the fearful penalty which our sins deserved, namely the death which is a separation from God.

Of course there is more to the Christian faith than the person and work of Christ. But these two truths are central. Of course too the divine-human person and sin-bearing death of Jesus (the Incarnation and the Atonement, to give them their theological names) contain mysteries beyond our understanding. We shall go on trying to penetrate their depths throughout our lives, and probably throughout eternity too. But still there is sufficient evidence for the straightforward facts of the gospel: the Son of God became human in Jesus of Nazareth, died for our sins on the cross, and was raised from the dead to vindicate him. It is these truths which qualify him to save us sinners; nobody else has ever had these qualifications.

Something to Consider

C stands for something to *Consider*, namely that Jesus Christ wants to be our Lord as well as our Saviour. He is in fact 'our Lord and Saviour Jesus Christ' (e.g. 2 Peter 3:18), and we have no liberty to cut him in two, responding to one half and rejecting the other. For he makes demands as well as offers. He offers us salvation (forgiveness and the liberating power of his Spirit); he demands our thoughtful and total allegiance.

In the language of the Alternative Service Book, we cannot say 'I turn to Christ' without going on to say 'I repent of my sins' and 'I renounce evil'. Moreover, repentance is not just remorse, a vague sense of regret and shame; it is a decisive turn from everything we know to be displeasing to God. Nor is it only negative and related to the past. It includes a determination to go Christ's way in the future, to become his disciple, to learn and obey his teaching (cf. Matthew 11:28–30). He told his contemporaries that they must count the cost of following him. He added that unless we are willing to put him first, before even our relations, our ambitions and our possessions, we cannot be his disciples (Luke 14: 25–35). He calls us to whole-hearted loyalty. Nothing less than this will do.

Something to Do

D stands for something to *Do*. The first three steps have all been taken in the mind. We admit we are sinners and need a Saviour. We believe Jesus Christ came and died to be our Saviour. We have considered that he wants to be our Lord as well. But we have not done anything about it yet. So now we need to ask what the crowd asked Peter on the Day of Pentecost: 'Brothers, what shall we do?' (Acts 2:37). Or more fully what the Philippian jailer asked Paul and Silas: 'Sirs, what must I do to be saved?' (Acts 16:30). The answer is that each of us needs to come to Jesus Christ personally and cry to him to have mercy upon us. It is one thing to admit that we need a Saviour. It is another to narrow our need down to Christ and believe that he came and died to be *the* Saviour we need. But then we have to ask him to be *our* Saviour and *our* Lord. It is this act of personal commitment which many people miss.

The verse which made it clear to me (nearly eighteen months *after* I had been confirmed, I am sorry to say) is understandably a favourite with many Christians. In it Jesus Christ is speaking, and this is what he says: 'Here I am! I stand at the door and knock. If anyone hears my voice and opens the door, I will come in and eat with him, and he with me' (Revelation 3:20). Jesus depicts himself as standing outside the closed door of our personality. He is knocking, in order to draw our attention to his presence and to signify his desire to come in. He then adds the promise that, if we open the door, he will come in and we will eat together. That is, the joy of our fellowship with each other will be so satisfying that it can only be compared to a feast.

Opening the door

Here, then, is the crucial question which we have been leading up to. Have we ever opened our door to Christ? Have we ever invited him in? This was exactly the question which I needed to have put to me.

For, intellectually speaking, I had believed in Jesus all my life, on the other side of the door. I had regularly struggled to say my prayers through the key-hole. I had even pushed pennies under the door in a vain attempt to pacify him. I had been baptized, yes and confirmed as well. I went to church, read my Bible, had high ideals, and tried to be good and do good. But all the time, often without realising it, I was holding Christ at arm's length, and keeping him outside. I knew that to open the door might have momentous consequences.

I am profoundly grateful to him for enabling me to open the door. Looking back now over more than fifty years, I realise that that simple step has changed the entire direction, course and quality of my life. At the same time, lest anyone should misconstrue what I have written, I feel the need to make three disclaimers. First, it is not necessary for 'conversion' or commitment to Christ to be accompanied by strong emotion. Because of our different temperaments and situations our experiences vary and we must not try to stereotype them. Speaking personally, I saw no flash of lightning and heard no peal of thunder. No electric shock passed through my body. I *felt* nothing. But the following day I knew that something inexplicable had happened to me, and as the days have passed into weeks, months, years and even decades, my relationship to Christ has steadily deepened and ripened.

Secondly, commitment to Christ is not the end. There is much to follow, as we seek to grow into maturity in Christ. But it is an indispensable beginning, to which you testify when you say at your confirmation 'I turn to Christ, I repent of my sins, I renounce evil'. Thirdly, it does not matter at all if, although you know you have turned to Christ, you do not know the date when you did so. Some do; others do not. What matters is not *when* but *whether* we have put our trust in Christ. Jesus called the beginning of our Christian life a second 'birth', and the analogy is helpful in many ways. For example, we are not conscious of our physical birth taking place, and would never have known our birthday if our parents had not told us. The reason we know we were born, even though we do not remember it, is that we are enjoying a life today which we know must have begun at birth. It is much the same with the new birth.

With these clarifications I come back to the basic question: on which side of the door is Jesus Christ? Is he inside or outside? If you are not sure, my advice to you is to make sure. It may be, as someone has put it, that you will be going over in ink what you have already written in pencil. But this issue is too important to leave in doubt. It may help you to get away and alone somewhere, where you will not be interrupted. You could perhaps re-read this section on 'Commitment to Christ'. Then, if you are ready to take the A-B-C-D steps which I have outlined, here is a prayer you could pray:

> Lord Jesus Christ, I admit that I have sinned against God and others, and have gone my own way. I repent of my self-centredness.
> I thank you for your great love in dying for me, for bearing in my place the penalty of my sins.
> Now I open the door of my heart to you. Come in, Lord Jesus. Come in as my Saviour, to cleanse and renew me. Come in as my Lord, to take control of me.
> And by your grace I will serve you faithfully, in fellowship with your other disciples, all my life. Amen.

---

[1] From *The Journal of John Wesley*, entries for 24th and 29th January, 1738.

[2] *Journal*, entry for 24th May, 1738.

Study guide to chapter 1

See general hints on p. 7

Basic

Questions

1. Although Christianity is not at heart a creed or code or cult, can you be a Christian without these things?
2. How would you explain the heart of Christianity to a friend who is not a Christian?
3. How and when do you think you became committed to Christ? Did you realize this at the time, or only later?

Promise

Christ's acceptance of us – Revelation 3:20; John 6:37.

Prayer

No 5 on p. 158 – for perseverance in the Christian life.

Extras

Bible study

Philippians 3:4–14.

In a group

Each person should introduce some basic information about themselves to the others by completing the sentence 'I am ...' in three different ways. Try to include facts about yourself which most of the others don't already know.

Response

Silently read again the prayer on p. 25 at the end of the chapter. Pause after each paragraph; do not move on to the next until you are sure you understand it and mean it. You may have said these or similar words to Jesus already; but it does no harm to confirm them and tell him again.

Check-up

Do you count yourself a committed Christian?

Suggestions for further reading

Note: When two or more book titles are listed, the first is the more introductory.

J.I. Packer, *I Want to be a Christian* (Kingsway, 1985). Basic teaching on the Apostle's Creed, baptism and conversion, the Lord's prayer, and the Ten Commandments.

John R.W. Stott, *Basic Christianity* (IVP, 1971). A study based on the person and work of Jesus.

Michael Green, *Baptism* (Hodder & Stoughton, 1987). Explains the different approaches to adult and infant baptism.

2. How to be Sure you are a Christian

Once we have opened the door to Jesus Christ and asked him to come in, can we be sure that he has done so? We have accepted him, but has he accepted us? Some people insist that we can never know, but can only hope for the best. Others warn us that to claim to know is to be guilty of pride and presumption. Yet knowledge is important, as an old Arabian proverb indicates:

He who knows not, and knows not that he knows not,
 is a fool: shun him.
He who knows not, and knows that he knows not,
 is simple: teach him.
He who knows, and knows not that he knows,
 is asleep: wake him.
But he who knows, and knows that he knows,
 is a wise man: follow him.

The New Testament clearly promises us an assurance which is not incompatible with humility. Open it anywhere, and it breathes a spirit of quiet, joyful confidence which is sadly lacking in many Christian churches today. 'I know whom I have believed', Paul wrote to Timothy, 'and am convinced that he is able to guard what I have entrusted to him for that day' (2 Timothy 1:12). John's letters in particular are full of affirmations about what 'we know'. For example, 'we know that we are children of God' (1 John 5:19). Indeed, John tells us that his main purpose in writing his first letter was to give his readers grounds on which to base their assurance: 'I write these things to you who believe in the name of the Son of God, so that you may know that you have eternal life' (1 John 5:13). This will sound very strange to those who think of eternal life as a synonym for heaven. But 'eternal life' means the life of the new era which Jesus inaugurated. It consists essentially of knowing God through Jesus Christ (John 17:3). It begins now and will be perfected in heaven. Christian assurance is about both.

There are several reasons why such an assurance is desirable. First, if God intends us to have and enjoy eternal life now (which Jesus undoubtedly taught), then he must also intend us to know that we have been given it. For we cannot enjoy what we do not know we have. Secondly, Scripture often promises us peace of mind. But if our conscience keeps nagging us, and we have no assurance of God's forgiveness, we can never be at peace. Thirdly, Christian assurance is a condition of helping other people. How can we show anybody else the way if we do not know it ourselves?

Accepting, then, that it is our Christian birthright not only to receive eternal life but also to know it, how can we come to this assurance? Like a camera tripod it rests on three legs, all of which need to be secure.

1. The work of God the Son

The first ground of our Christian assurance is the work of salvation which Jesus Christ accomplished when he died on the cross. We need to ask ourselves about the object of our faith. If we believe we have been forgiven, and if we hope to go to heaven when we die, what are we trusting in for these things? If we reply, as some do, 'Well, I lead a good life, I go to church regularly, I ...', we need go no further. The first word of our reply was 'I'. Exactly! We are evidently still trusting in ourselves. There is no assurance of salvation that way, only of judgment. If, on the other hand, we reply to the question with the single word 'Christ', that is, 'the Saviour who died for me is my only hope', then we may know that we have been 'ransomed, healed, restored, forgiven'. The hymn puts it well:

My hope is built on nothing less
than Jesus' blood and righteousness;
no merit of my own I claim,
but wholly trust in Jesus' name.
   On Christ, the solid rock, I stand –
   all other ground is sinking sand.

One reason why our own works are like 'sinking sand' is that they are not finished until we die. So we can never know if we have done enough, or rather we can know that we have not and could not. By contrast, Jesus Christ is like 'solid rock' because his work is finished. When he had borne our sins, he cried with a loud voice 'It is finished' (John 19:30). Indeed, when he 'had offered for all time one sacrifice for sins, he sat down at the right hand of God' (Hebrews 10:12). Sitting is the posture of rest and God's right hand is the place of honour; both are due to Christ's completion of the work he came to do.

'It is finished'

This is the truth which broke into the mind of a young man called Hudson Taylor who was later to qualify as a doctor and to found the China Inland Mission (now 'Overseas Missionary Fellowship'). He was seventeen years old at the time and on holiday. His mother was away from home and, although he did not know this at the time, she was praying earnestly for his conversion. He looked idly through his father's library and then picked up a tract and read it. Here is his own account of what happened:

I ... was struck with the phrase 'the finished work of Christ'.... Immediately the words 'It is finished' suggested themselves to my mind. What was finished? And I at once replied, 'A full and perfect atonement and satisfaction for sin. The debt was paid for our sins, and not for ours only, but also for the sins of the whole world.' Then came the further thought, 'If the whole work was finished and the whole debt paid, what is there left for me to do?' And with this dawned the joyful conviction, as light was flashed into my soul by the Holy Spirit, that there was nothing in the world to be done but to fall down on one's knees, and accepting this Saviour and his salvation praise him for evermore.[1]

So the first and fundamental ground of our assurance, because it is the sole ground of our salvation, is 'the finished work of Christ'. Whenever our conscience accuses us, and we feel burdened with guilt, we need to look away from ourselves to Christ crucified. Then again we will have peace. For our acceptance with God depends not on ourselves and what we could ever do, but entirely on Christ and what he has done once and for all on the cross.

2. The word of God the Father

Granted that the essential ground of our Christian assurance is the finished work of God the Son, how can we know that when we put our trust in Christ crucified we receive forgiveness and a new life? Because God says so. The sure word of God the Father endorses and guarantees the finished work of God the Son. John put it like this: 'We accept man's testimony, but God's testimony is greater because it is the testimony of God, which he has given about his Son ... He who has the Son has life; he who does not have the Son of God does not have life' (1 John 5:9,12). The Father has accepted the Son's sacrifice for our sins. He has publicly demonstrated his approval of it by raising him from the dead and setting him at his right hand. And now he promises to give eternal life to those who trust in him. It is not presumptuous to believe God's word. Would it not rather be presumptuous to doubt it? 'Anyone who does not believe God has made him out to be a liar, because he has not believed the testimony God has given about his Son. And this is the testimony: God has given us eternal life, and this life is in his Son' (1 John 5:10, 11).

If, then, our assurance rests above all on God's word about Christ's work, it does not depend primarily on our feelings. Feelings are an unreliable index to our true spiritual condition. They go up and down like a seesaw, to and fro like the swings. They rise and fall like a barometer, and ebb and flow like the tides of the sea. We are such psychosomatic creatures that our mood is affected by our liver, kidneys and spleen. Our feelings also reflect the state of our bank balance, the proximity of our holidays, and the weight of our worries and responsibilities. So the Bible and Christian biographies contain many stories of God's people, who have learned to distrust their feelings and to trust God's promises instead. Our feelings fluctuate, but 'the word of the Lord stands for ever' (1 Peter 1:25, quoting Isaiah 40:8).

God's promises

Wise Christians learn by heart as many as possible of God's 'very great and precious promises' (2 Peter 1:4), and store them up in their memory. Then, in times of anxiety, indecision, loneliness or temptation, we will be able to recall an appropriate promise, hold on to it and focus our mind on it. I have listed a number of God's promises at the end of this chapter. It may be helpful to begin by committing these to memory. Mind you, we must be conscientious in noting the circumstances in which God made each promise, and not wrench it out of its context. That was the mistake our Victorian

John Bunyan (1628–1688), author of the classic *Pilgrim's Progress*.

ancestors made with their 'promise boxes'. These contained biblical promises, each of which had been printed on a slip of paper, rolled up like a baby scroll and tied with a little ribbon. Then Christians would pick out a promise at random, irrespective of the original situation in which it had been made. In contrast to this haphazard method, we must ensure with integrity that a promise may legitimately be applied to our position. Then we shall be able, humbly but confidently, to claim it for ourselves and so 'to imitate those who through faith and patience inherit what has been promised' (Hebrews 6:12).

This is the lesson which Christian learned in Bunyan's great allegory *Pilgrim's Progress*. Christian and his companion Hopeful found themselves one day in Doubting Castle, as prisoners of the cruel and pitiless Giant Despair. Days passed, and there seemed to be no possibility of escape, until one night as they prayed, Christian made a wonderful discovery, which he immediately shared with Hopeful: 'What a fool am I thus to lie in a stinking dungeon when I may as well walk at liberty! I have a key in my bosom called Promise that will, I am persuaded, open any lock in Doubting Castle.' Using this key, 'the door flew open with ease' and the prisoners 'escaped with speed'.

Knowing the weakness of our faith, God has not given us his gospel promises in bare or naked form; he has 'clothed' them in visible, tangible signs, which are commonly called 'sacraments'. One of their chief purposes is to elicit, educate and strengthen our faith. Probably the best definition of a sacrament is that found in the Catechism of the 1662 Prayer Book. According to this, it is –

an outward and visible sign of an inward and spiritual grace given unto us, ordained by Christ himself, as a means whereby we receive the same, and a pledge to assure us thereof.

The latter phrases will be discussed in a later chapter. What is important at this point is the opening clause of the definition, which could perhaps be simplified into saying that a sacrament is 'an outward and visible sign of an inward and spiritual gift of God'. Similarly, one of the sixteenth century Homilies (sample sermons provided for the clergy) calls the sacraments 'visible signs to which are annexed promises'. More simply still, the sacraments are 'visible words' (Augustine), dramatized promises.

We human beings also use signs to convey and confirm our promises. 'I will forgive all the past and be your friend', someone says to his former enemy, and holds out his hand in token of his offer of reconciliation. 'I love you', a husband says to his wife, and covers her with kisses. 'I will always serve my country', a soldier says to himself, as he salutes the flag. Our everyday life is enriched by many such outward and visible signs. We pledge our friendship with a handshake, our love with a kiss, our loyalty with a salute.

Two great sacraments

Similarly, the two great sacraments of the gospel are so called because they dramatize the promises of the gospel and are intended to stimulate our faith to lay hold of them. In baptism the outward and visible sign is water. It stands for the 'heavenly washing' (a prayer book expression), or inward cleansing from sin through the blood of Christ, which we all need and which is offered to us in the gospel, together with the promise of the Holy Spirit. It also sets forth our sharing in the death and resurrection of Jesus (Romans 6:3,4). Indeed, one of the main reasons why some churches prefer to baptize by immersion is that this readily symbolizes our going down into death and burial with Christ and our rising again with him to a new life. As a matter of fact, the earliest pictures of the baptism of Jesus by John the Baptist portray them standing waist-deep in the River Jordan, while John pours water over Jesus' head. Personally, I wish we could recover this combination of immersion and pouring, for together they would visibly symbolize (1) our death and resurrection with Christ, (2) our being made clean from sin, and (3) our being baptized by the outpoured Holy Spirit. The water signifies all these gospel promises and so stimulates our faith to claim them for ourselves.

In the case of infant baptism,[2] the water is a visible sign and seal of the same blessings. It does not confer them upon children automatically, any more than it does on adults. What it does is to promise forgiveness and the gift of the Spirit to them, yet only after they have been represented in the service as declaring their repentance and faith through their sponsors, and only on the understanding that they will later personally repent and believe. The validity of their baptism depends on this. Only then will they enter into the enjoyment of the salvation promised to them in their baptism. This is the purpose of their confirmation. Confirmation is not a sacrament of the gospel, for it was not instituted by Christ, as baptism and Holy Communion were. Nevertheless it has an outward and visible sign. The laying on of the bishop's hands, as we have seen, is like the stretching forth of God's hands towards those being confirmed in welcome, acceptance and fatherly friendship.

In the Holy Communion, the second gospel sacrament, the outward and visible signs are bread and wine. They are tangible emblems of the death of Jesus Christ. The bread is broken and the wine poured out in order to exhibit the giving of his body and the shedding of his blood in his death on the cross. Then the broken bread is eaten and the poured wine is drunk to indicate our personal share in what he did for us when he died.

Once and for all
'What happens if and when I sin?', a bewildered Christian sometimes asks. 'Do I have to receive Christ all over again?' No, indeed not. When we opened the door to Christ, and Christ came in, God accepted us ('justified us' is the biblical term) and gave us his Spirit once and for all. That is why we are baptized only once. At the same time, although we are justified once and for all, we need to be forgiven every day. That is why we come to Holy Communion often. Jesus probably had this distinction in mind when he washed his apostles' feet. Peter said to him, 'Lord, not just my feet but my hands and my head as well!' To this Jesus replied: 'A person who has had

a bath needs only to wash his feet; his whole body is clean' (John 13:9,10). In other words, when we first come to Christ, we receive the 'bath' of justification. We are made clean all over. But day by day our feet get dirty, and we need the foot-washing of a daily forgiveness. If we fall, then, we need to fall on our knees, and ask God's forgiveness at once. There is no need to wait until the next time we go to church, or even until we pray before going to bed. Rather we should confess our sin immediately, remembering and claiming this wonderful promise: 'If we confess our sins, God is faithful and just and will forgive us our sins and purify us from all unrighteousness' (1 John 1:9). Then too the bread and wine of Communion will bring us a repeated visible assurance of our forgiveness through Christ's death, as our baptism (and confirmation) assured us once for all that we had been justified.

Thank God for his promises of salvation, and for the sacraments which dramatize them; they are the reassuring kisses of his love.

3. The witness of God the Holy Spirit

If our Christian assurance rests primarily on the finished work of God the Son, who died for our sins, and secondarily on the word of God the Father, who promises salvation to those who trust in Christ crucified, its third ground is the witness – both internal and external – of God the Holy Spirit.

Consider his inward witness first. The wisdom of mistrusting our feelings has already been mentioned. Because they fluctuate, they are an unreliable guide to our spiritual state. Yet feelings have a place in our Christian assurance – not the fickle flutters of a shallow emotion, but the steady increase of a deepening conviction. Of this the New Testament speaks. It is the work of the indwelling Spirit. We sometimes over-emphasize his work of pricking our conscience and convicting us of sin. He certainly does this. But it is also his gracious work to pacify our consciences, calm our fears, and counter our doubts with his gentle reassurance.

Paul alludes twice in his Letter to the Romans to this inward work of the Spirit. In Romans 5:5 he writes that 'God has poured out his love into our hearts by the Holy Spirit, whom he has given us', and in Romans 8:16 that 'the Spirit himself testifies with our spirit that we are God's children', especially when he prompts us to cry 'Abba,

Father' (verse 15). Do we sometimes become profoundly aware that God has set his love upon us, that the old tension and friction between him and us has given place to reconciliation, and that his arms enfold and uphold us? It is the witness of the Spirit. Do we sense in prayer that we are in right relationship with God, that his smile is upon us, that he is our Father and we are his children? Again, it is the witness of the Spirit. He pours God's love into our hearts and he makes God's fatherhood a reality to us. Sometimes his witness is quiet and undemonstrative. At other times, as Christian people in different ages and cultures have testified, it can become an overwhelming experience of his presence and mercy.

Character and conduct
If the internal witness of the Spirit is in our hearts, his external witness is in our character and conduct. When Paul listed nine of the chief qualities of Christlikeness ('love, joy, peace, patience, kindness, goodness, faithfulness, gentleness and self-control'), he called them 'the fruit of the Spirit', which he causes to ripen in our lives (Galatians 5:22, 23). He thus likens the Spirit to a gardener and us to his garden. If the garden is full of noxious weeds, we may be sure that the divine gardener is absent. But if the good fruits of Christian holiness appear, we may know that it is he who is causing them to grow. 'By their fruit you will recognise them', Jesus said (Matthew 7:16).

John makes the same point in different words. We noted earlier that his purpose in writing his first letter was to strengthen the assurance of true Christians; it was also to undermine false or counterfeit assurance. The way he did it was to bring together three tests and to keep applying them with rigour. We know that we know God, he wrote, because we believe in his Son Jesus Christ, because we obey his commands, and because we love one another. Thus truth, obedience and love are the tests. Conversely (John pulls no punches), if we claim to know God but deny Christ, disobey his commands and hate our brothers, we are 'liars' (1 John 1:6; 2:4, 22; 4:20).

It is clear, then, that God wants his children to be sure that they belong to him, and does not want us to remain in doubt and uncertainty. So much so, that each of the three persons of the Trinity contributes to our assurance. The witness of God the Holy Spirit confirms the word of God the Father concerning the work of God the Son. The three strong legs of this tripod make it very steady indeed.

God's promises

Of Christ's acceptance of us	Revelation 3:20; John 6:37.
Of eternal life	John 5:24; 6:47; 10:28.
Of daily forgiveness	1 John 1:9.
Of Christ's abiding presence	Matthew 28:20; Heb. 13:5, 6.
Of divine wisdom	James 1:5.
Of strength in temptation	1 Corinthians 10:13.
Of answered prayer	John 15:7.
Of peace of mind	Philippians 4:6, 7.
Of God's faithfulness	Joshua 1:9; Isaiah 41:10.
Of God's guidance	Psalms 32:8, 9.
Of helping others	John 7:38.

---

[1] Dr. and Mrs. Howard Taylor, *Hudson Taylor in Early Years* (1911), pp. 66–67. See also Roger Steer, *J. Hudson Taylor: A Man in Christ* (OMF, 1990), p. 6.

[2] I do not think this is the place for a full defence of the practice of infant baptism. For those who wish to weigh the arguments for it, I recommend *Baptism* by Michael Green (Hodder & Stoughton, 1987) and *Believing in Baptism* by Gordon Kuhrt (Mowbray, 1987). I make only three points. (1) The practice of infant baptism is defensible only in the case of the children of professing Christian parents. (2) It makes sense when we remember that the God of the Bible thinks and works in relation to families. The Old Testament practice of circumcision shows that believers' children are in God's covenant (Genesis 17), Jesus' attitude and teaching show that they are in God's kingdom (Mark 10:13–16), and Paul's statement that they are 'holy' shows that they are in God's church (1 Corinthains 7:12–14). If this is their status by birth, it seems right to add the sign of it, which is baptism. Further, the early 'household' baptisms (e.g. Acts 16:15, 33; 1 Corinthians 1:16) almost certainly included children, since *oikos* and *oikia*, meaning 'household', were often synonyms for a family with children (cf. 1 Timothy 3:4, 5). (3) The case for infant baptism, though defensible from Scripture, cannot be proved from Scripture. It must not be demanded, therefore. Churches should not separate over it, but rather recognize each other's baptisms. In future united churches, parents should be given liberty, whether to ask for the baptism of their children or not.

Study guide to chapter 2
See general hints on p. 7

Basic

Questions
1. How would you answer someone who says, 'It is arrogant to say you *know* you've got eternal life and will go to heaven'?
2. How would you answer someone who says, 'I think I'm a Christian, but (a) I'm not a very good one, and (b) sometimes I doubt whether it is all true'?
3. How far are you aware of the witness of the Holy Spirit (both internal and external, see pp. 34–35) in your life?

Promise
Eternal life – John 5:24; 6:47; 10:28.

Prayer
No 4 on p. 158 – for those who lack assurance.

Extras

Bible study
1 John 3:11–24

In a group
Go round the circle, each completing the sentence 'I'm glad I'm a Christian because ...' with just one reason. Don't worry if you repeat what someone else said. How do you feel after hearing everyone else's reasons? If you can think of even more reasons, go round a second time.

Response
On a piece of paper list five of the things you feel most sure of in life (e.g. that you are alive or that your parents love you). Reflect silently on each one for a few moments – how and why are you so sure? – and then give thanks to God.

Check-up
Are you sure you are a Christian? How?
(If relevant) Do you feel ready to go ahead with preparing to be confirmed?

Suggestions for further reading
A helpful chapter, from a nineteenth-century book that remains evergreen, is that on 'Assurance' in J.C. Ryle's *Holiness* (Evangelical Press reprint, 1979).
Alister McGrath, *Doubt* (IVP, 1990). Offers suggestions for handling specific doubts and anxieties which Christians experience.

3. How to Grow as a Christian

Our thankful assurance that God has welcomed and forgiven us, and given us his Spirit, cannot in any way be made an excuse for complacency. Rather the reverse. It gives us a desire to go on with Christ and to grow into Christian maturity.

The need for growth

Christian growth is illustrated in the New Testament by several different metaphors. One of the most important introduces us to the words 'justification' and 'sanctification', and to the clear distinction which Scripture draws between them.

Justification describes the position of acceptance with God which he gives us when we trust in Christ as our Saviour. It is a legal term, borrowed from the law courts, and its opposite is condemnation. To justify is to acquit, to declare an accused person to be just, not guilty. So the divine judge, because his Son has borne our condemnation, justifies us, pronouncing us righteous in his sight. 'Therefore, there is now no condemnation for those who are in Christ Jesus' (Romans 8:1).

Sanctification, on the other hand, describes the process by which justified Christians are changed into the likeness of Christ. When God justifies us, he *declares* us righteous through Christ's death for us; when he sanctifies us, he *makes* us righteous through the power of his Holy Spirit within us. Justification concerns our outward status of acceptance with God; sanctification concerns our inward growth in holiness of character. Further, whereas our justification is sudden and complete, so that we shall never be more justified than we were on the day of our conversion, our sanctification is gradual and incomplete. It takes a few moments only in court for a judge to pronounce his verdict and for the accused to be acquitted; it takes a lifetime even to approach Christlikeness.

Born again

The New Testament authors have another way of teaching this distinction between the beginning and the continuing of our Christian life. They tell us that, when Jesus Christ becomes our Saviour and Lord, we are not only justified but also regenerated or born again. The metaphor has changed. We have left the law court and entered the maternity ward. What we see before us now is not a prisoner who has just been acquitted, but a baby who has just been born. How long does it take for a baby to be born? Only a few minutes. Of course months of preparation precede birth, and labour may last several hours, but the birth itself is a sudden and almost instantaneous crisis. A new, independent life emerges into the world. Although, however, it takes a baby only a few minutes to be born, it takes perhaps twenty-five years for a person to reach full physical and emotional maturity. The dramatic crisis of birth is followed by the laborious process of growth. So then, what sanctification is to justification, growth is to birth. Justification and regeneration take place together the moment we are united to Christ by faith, whether we are conscious of what is happening or not; sanctification and growth, on the other hand, take time.

God's general purpose is that all human beings should grow up physically, mentally and emotionally. It is very sad when people are retarded in any of these areas. Equally sad is arrested spiritual growth. Hundreds of people in the church have never graduated from the nursery. They suffer (to borrow a Freudian term) from 'infantile regression' of the spirit. Paul called them 'mere infants in Christ' (1 Corinthians 3:1), whereas his ambition was to 'present everyone perfect (better, 'mature') in Christ' (Colossians 1:28).

Normally, it is a matter of pride to children to grow up. I can still remember the exultation I felt on the day I first got out of my pram and was allowed to walk; and my pride when I first exchanged shorts for long trousers knew no bounds! It is a very healthy sign when new-born Christians exhibit the same eagerness to grow into maturity. Confirmation is an important milestone for all of us, especially if we regard it as a new beginning, rather than as an end. It reminds me of those stirring words spoken by Winston Churchill in

1942, just after the successful conclusion of the Battle of El Alamein in Egypt. Rommel and the Afrika Korps had been routed; 30,000 prisoners had been taken; and the first victory of the war had been won. Invited to attend the new Lord Mayor's luncheon banquet at the Mansion House, the Prime Minster said: 'Gentlemen, this is not the end. It is not even the beginning of the end. But it is perhaps the end of the beginning.' Loud cheers greeted his memorable statement. Whether we are thinking of our conversion, our baptism or our confirmation, I hope we can be equally enthusiastic in celebrating it as the beginning of a new life.

The areas of growth

The New Testament writers are quite precise about the areas in which they expect Christian growth to take place. They specify four main ones.

Faith

First, we are to *grow in faith*. Of course, faith is an indispensable characteristic of Christians. They are often identified as 'believers', and Jesus called a disciple 'one who believes in me'. But what is faith? It is neither credulity nor superstition. Faith is trust. Christians are believers because they have put their trust in Jesus Christ as their Saviour, and because they take God at his word and rely on his promises. This shows why faith, though it goes beyond reason, is never against reason. The reasonableness of trust depends on the trustworthiness of the person being trusted, and no more trustworthy person exists than the God who has revealed himself in Christ.

Faith is not a static thing, however; it should be living and growing. Once Jesus rebuked his apostles as 'you of little faith', although he added later that if they had a faith as small as a mustard seed, they could accomplish great things for God (Matthew 6:8; 17:20). On another occasion they came to Jesus and said: 'Increase our faith' (Luke 17:5). And twice he spoke of the 'great faith' shown even by Gentiles (Mathew 8:10; 15:28). It is plain from these texts that there are degrees to faith. It is little at first, but can increase until it becomes strong. As we read the Bible, meditate on the absolute reliability of God's character, and put his promises to the test, our faith will ripen. What Paul wrote to the Thessalonians ought to be true of all of us: 'your faith is growing more and more' (2 Thessalonians 1:3).

Love

Secondly, we are to *grow in love*. Jesus summarized the law by bringing together the Old Testament commands to love God with all our being and to love our neighbour as ourselves (Deuteronomy 6:5; Leviticus 19:18; Mark 12:28–31), and Paul declared love to be 'the fulfilment of the law' (Romans 13:10). He added that love is greater than faith and hope, indeed the greatest of all virtues (1 Corinthians 13:13). And the reason for this is that God is love and has set his love upon us. Indeed, 'we love because he first loved us' (1 John 4:7–12, 19).

Yet we have to confess that neither Christians nor churches are always conspicuous for the quality of their loving. Paul had to declare the Corinthians worldly and babyish because there was jealousy and quarrelling among them (1 Corinthians 3:1–3), and one wonders how he would evaluate our churches today. Generally speaking, there is affability and a certain degree of *bonhomie*, but these things often conceal rivalries and factions, and there is comparatively little sacrificial, serving, supportive love for each other, let alone for the needy world outside. Without doubt we need to hear and heed another of Paul's words to the Thessalonians: 'in fact, you do love all the brothers ... Yet we urge you, brothers, to do so more and more' (1 Thessalonians 4:10). He also prayed that their love would 'increase and overflow' (1 Thessalonians 3:12).

Knowledge

Thirdly, we are to *grow in knowledge*. Christianity lays great emphasis on the importance of knowledge, rebukes anti-intellectualism for the negative, paralysing thing it is, and traces many of our problems to our ignorance. Whenever the heart is full and the head is empty, dangerous fanaticisms arise. Nobody has stressed this more than Paul. 'In your thinking be adults', he wrote to the Corinthians (1 Corinthians 14:20). He began many sentences with the refrain 'I want you to know' or 'I do not want you to be ignorant' (e.g. 1 Thessalonians 4:13), and he sometimes expostulated 'but don't you know ... ?', with the implication that if his readers did know, they would behave differently. It is hardly surprising, therefore, that the burden of his prayers for his converts was 'that you may know' (e.g. Ephesians 1:18; 3:19; Philippians 1:10; Colossians 1:9).

At the same time, we need to remember that the Hebrew concept of knowing was never purely intellectual. It went beyond 'understanding' to 'experiencing'. This is specially true of the knowledge of God. We have already seen that knowing God in Jesus Christ, which is the essence of being a Christian, means a living, personal relationship to him. Like all relationships it should be dynamic and growing as well. If it is not nurtured, it will wither and die. It is noteworthy, therefore, that in the very passage in which Paul affirms 'the surpassing greatness of knowing Christ Jesus my Lord' he also writes that his chief ambition is 'to know Christ', and to enter ever more deeply into his sufferings, his death and his resurrection power (Philippians 3:8,10). What he desires for himself he naturally desires for others too, and prays that they may be continuously 'growing in the knowledge of God' (Colossians 1:10). Peter shares the same longing. He urges his readers to 'grow in the grace and knowledge of our Lord and Saviour Jesus Christ' (2 Peter 3:18).

Holiness

Fourthly, we are to *grow in holiness*. Growth in holiness is the process called 'sanctification', about which we began to think near the beginning of this chapter. Paul gives us a most enlightening statement of it: 'And we, who with unveiled faces all reflect the Lord's glory, are being transformed into his likeness with ever-increasing glory, which comes from the Lord, who is the Spirit' (2 Corinthians 3:18). We can learn at least four vital lessons from this verse.

(1) Holiness is Christlikeness, and sanctification is the process of being transformed (the verb *metamorphoō* is used of Jesus' transfiguration) into his image. I love the chorus which children sometimes sing: 'Like Jesus, like Jesus, I want to be like Jesus. I love him so, I want to grow like Jesus day by day'.

(2) Sanctification is a gradual process, as is clear both from the present continuous tense ('are being transformed') and from the expression 'ever-increasing glory'. Although indeed some bad habits drop away instantaneously when Christ comes into our life, yet we do not become mature in the twinkling of an eye. Tempers are not tamed, nor passions controlled, nor is selfishness conquered

The carpenter provides a rich metaphor for God's work.

in a moment. Instead, we are urged to learn to 'please God ... more and more' (1 Thessalonians 4:1).

(3) Holiness is the work of the Holy Spirit. Being himself inherently holy, he is concerned to promote our holiness. The secret of sanctification is not that we struggle to live like Christ, but that Christ comes by his Spirit to live in us. As Bishop William Wand of London once expressed it, 'Christian character is not attained by the laborious acquisition of virtues from without, but by the expression of the Christ-life from within'.[1]

(4) If the Holy Spirit is to do his work of transforming us 'with ever-increasing glory', our part is 'with unveiled faces' to contemplate and so reflect the glory of the Lord. And since it is in the Scriptures that his glory is most clearly revealed, our 'contemplation' will mean seeking him there in order to worship him.

The divine potter

So, to change the metaphor, we must let the divine potter have his way with us, so that he can fashion out of the poor clay of our fallen nature a beautiful vessel fit for his use. Or, changing the metaphor again, we may say that the carpenter from Nazareth is still busy with his tools. Now by the chisel of pain, now by the hammer of affliction, now by the plane of adverse circumstance, as well as through experiences of joy, he is shaping us into an instrument of righteousness. It is well expressed in a quaint old prayer:

O Jesus, Master-Carpenter of Nazareth, who on the cross through wood and nails hast wrought man's full salvation, wield well thy tools in this thy workshop, that we who come to thee rough-hewn, may be fashioned into a truer beauty by thy hand, who with the Father and the Holy Spirit livest and reignest, one God, world without end.[2]

So I venture to urge you to be patient, but determined. Do not lose heart. Watch the discipline of your Christian life. Be diligent in daily prayer and Bible-reading, in church-going and attendance at the Lord's Supper. Make good use of your Sundays. Read helpful books. Seek out Christian friends. Get busy in some form of service. Never leave your sins unconfessed and unforgiven. Never allow a pocket of resistance to arise in your heart. Above all, yield yourself without reserve each day to the power of the Holy Spirit who is within you. Then step by step you will advance along the road of holiness, and grow towards full spiritual maturity.

The means of growth

In Part III of this book we will be considering the main 'means of grace', that is, the channels God has chosen through which his grace comes to us and strengthens us. Here I will just anticipate briefly what I will be elaborating there. By what means can we ensure our Christian growth? If we take the analogy of a growing child (which is much used by the New Testament writers), we have our answer at once. Although many factors combine to foster and safeguard the healthy growth of a child, two stand out in importance from the rest. The greatest single condition of children's *physical* growth is the regularity of a right diet, and of their *psychological* development the security of a happy home. Each has its parallel in the maturity of those whom the Bible calls 'infants in Christ'.

Take the question of diet first. For babies this is of course milk, offered (at least according to ancient tradition) every four hours. Nowadays mothers tend to feed their babies less by the clock than by need and demand. Florence Nightingale, the pioneer of modern nursing, belonged to the old school, however. In her book *Notes on Nursing* (1859) the final chapter is entitled 'Minding Baby'. She wrote it particularly for the eldest daughter of the family. She gives seven conditions for the healthy growth of a child, the fourth of which being 'feeding it with proper food at regular times'. She explains:

You must be very careful about its food; about being strict to the minute for feeding it; not giving it too much at a time (if baby is sick after its food, you have given it too much). Neither must it be under-fed. Above all, never give it any unwholesome food ... Baby who is weaned requires to be fed often, regularly, and not too much at a time. I know a mother whose baby was in great danger one day from convulsions. It was about a year old. She said she had wished to go to church; and so, before going, had given it its three meals in one. Was it any wonder that the poor little thing had convulsions?

Spiritual milk

From the practical wisdom of Florence Nightingale we turn to an instruction of the apostle Peter: 'Like newborn babies, crave pure spiritual milk, so that by it you may grow up in your salvation, now that you have tasted that the Lord is good' (1 Peter 2:2, 3). What is this 'pure milk' which newborn Christians need? Peter calls it *logikos*, which could mean 'spiritual' (i.e. metaphorical in contrast to literal) or 'rational' (food for the mind as opposed to the body). Or it could be translated, as in the Authorised Version, 'the sincere milk of the word'. In this case Peter is taking up the references he has just made to 'the living and enduring word of God' (1 Peter 2:23, 24), and is affirming that the same word of God, which is the instru-ment of spiritual birth (1 Peter 1:23), is also the instrument of spiritual growth (1 Peter 2:2).

Certainly God's word is often likened to food for the soul. Its simple teaching is like milk and its deeper truth like solid food (1 Corinthians 3:2; Hebrews 5:11–14). Its precepts and promises are 'sweeter than honey and the honeycomb' (Psalms 19:10; cf. 119:103). As we 'eat' them, they become the joy and delight of our hearts (Jeremiah 15:16). That is why we pray each year on 'Bible Sunday' (the second Sunday in Advent) that we may 'read, mark, learn and inwardly digest' the Scriptures, and why the unknown author of the apocryphal *Epistle of Barnabas*, who was much given to far-fetched allegorizations, described God's people as 'those who know that meditation is a work of gladness and who chew the cud of the word of the Lord'!

I shall have more to say later about the importance of methodical Bible reading, but it is not too early for me to lay stress now on the daily discipline of this practice. It is the regularity which matters if we are to make steady spiritual progress. If we gorge ourselves with Scripture on Sundays, or at some Christian convention or conference, and hardly feed on it at all otherwise, we are likely to have spiritual convulsions like the baby in Florence Nightingale's story. A good appetite is a reliable sign of spiritual health, as of physical. It is certainly true of children. We have all seen the scarlet-faced, screaming protest of a baby whose meal is overdue. This is what Peter had in mind when he told us to 'crave' our spiritual milk. One commentator writes of 'the ardour of a suckled child'. We have already 'tasted' the Lord's goodness (1 Peter 2:3), Peter writes; so now let us 'thirst' after him in his word (1 Peter 2:2). Only then will we 'grow up in our salvation', or, as it literally means, 'into salvation'. By 'salvation' here the apostle must be referring to sanctification, and especially to ridding ourselves of symptoms of immaturity like 'malice, deceit, hypocrisy, envy and slander' which he has mentioned (1 Peter 2:1).

Happy home

From the regularity of a right diet we turn to the security of a happy home. Psychologists and psychotherapists talk a great deal about the influence (for good or ill) of our home surroundings on our early emotional development. God's purpose is that children should be born into, and nurtured within, a stable and loving family. His ideal for newborn Christians is the same. Many of us have altogether too individualistic a concept of the Christian life. 'Christ died for me', we say. And that is true and biblical (Galatians 2:20). But it is not the whole truth. He also died 'for us ... to purify for himself a people that are his very own' (Titus 2:14). So when we are born again, we are not born in a spiritual isolation hospital! On the contrary, we are born into the family of God. He becomes our heavenly father, Jesus Christ our elder brother, and all other Christians throughout the world, irrespective of their place and race, nation and denomination, our brothers and sisters in Christ. If, therefore, we hope to grow up into healthy Christian maturity, we can do so only in the family of God. Church membership is neither a luxury, nor an optional extra; it is a duty and a necessity. To try to dispense with it is as much a grievous folly as a sin.

In saying this, I am of course assuming that our church is a genuine fellowship, whose members are bound together in mutual support and care. But all too often this kind of life and love is missing. Someone who drew attention to this was Dr. Hobart Mowrer, the late Emeritus Professor of Psychiatry in the University of Illinois. He was a well-known critic of Freud, a promoter of what he called 'integrity groups', and a thinker who stressed the contractual obligations implicit in all our relationships. A few years ago he kindly gave time to some friends and me, who wanted to ask him some questions. He was not a Christian, he told us, nor even a theist. He had what he called 'a lover's quarrel with the church'. What did he mean? He complained that the church had failed him when he was a teenager, and continued to fail his patients. How so? we asked. 'Because', he replied, 'the church has never learned the secret of community'. It is perhaps the most damaging criticism of the church which I have ever heard. For the church *is* community, the new community of Jesus Christ. And many churches *have* learned the meaning and the demands of a community of love. But others have not. In that Professor Mowrer was right. At all events, I doubt if anybody has ever developed into a balanced or mature follower of Jesus Christ who has not worshipped and (as our American friends say) 'fellowshipped' in a regular and committed way with other believers. Confirmation is the door into full and active membership of the church.

These, then, are the major conditions of spiritual progress. If you are about to be confirmed, or have recently been confirmed, I want to urge you to take them to heart. Do not be content with a static Christian life. Determine rather to grow in faith and love, in knowledge and holiness. And in order to do so, be disciplined in seeking God daily through Bible reading and prayer, and throw yourself wholeheartedly into the life, worship, fellowship and witness of your church. For these things will greatly encourage and strengthen you, and your spiritual growth will be natural and steady.

---

[1] *The London Churchman*, August 1956.
[2] Attributed to Hal Pink, in *A Treasury of Prayers and Praises for use in Toc H* (1945).

Study guide to chapter 3

See general hints on p. 7

Basic

Questions

1. What score out of 10 would you give yourself on each of the four areas of growth in this chapter?

2. How might you be able to develop your spiritual 'diet' and 'home' (see pp. 44–47) to help strengthen your weakest area(s) of growth?

3. What advice would you give to new Christians to help them grow and not stagnate?

Promise

Daily forgiveness – 1 John 1:9.

Prayers

No 6 on p. 158 – for growth in Christian understanding.
No 7 on p. 158 – for growth in holiness.

Extras

Bible study

2 Peter 1:3–11

In a group

Take it in turns to talk about 'one thing I have (re)learned or (re)discovered in the past week'. It does not have to be profound or even 'spiritual'; any fresh facet, truth, experience or skill will have led you to develop in some way as a person. Say a little about how you learned it and what the effect on you has been.

Response

Buy a small plant – or take fresh notice of it, if you already have one. What insights into Christian growth can you learn from the way it grows?

Check-up

Are you growing as a Christian? Or have you got stuck?

Suggestions for further reading

John White, *The Fight* (IVP, 1977). A handbook on Christian living.
Dietrich Bonhoeffer, *The Cost of Discipleship* (1948; SCM reprint, 1982). A classic critique of the doctrine of 'cheap grace' and a call to commitment and suffering in authentic discipleship.

Christian Belief

We turn now from Christian beginnings to Christian belief. We have already seen how important it is for us to know what we believe and why we believe it. The preface to the old Confirmation Service (1662) says that 'none hereafter shall be confirmed, but such as can say the Creed ...'. We do not actually have to say it in the service, but we ought to know it by heart and have a good understanding of it too.

4. Belief in God the Father

The word 'creed' is derived from the Latin verb *credo*, I believe. In fact, the Creed begins with these words. Christian creeds, then, are summaries of Christian belief, and people started making them at a very early date, particularly to help in the instruction of converts. There are even traces of short creeds in the New Testament (e.g. 1 Timothy 3:16).

Three creeds are included in the Book of Common Prayer.

First, there is *the Apostles' Creed*, which is said at Morning and Evening Prayer. It is to this that people are usually referring when they talk simply of 'the Creed'. It was not composed by the twelve apostles and did not reach its final form until the middle of the eighth century AD, but a number of its clauses have been traced back to the second century. It is rightly called the Apostles' Creed, however, because it states concisely the teaching which the apostles give us in the New Testament about God.

Secondly, there is *the Nicene Creed*, which is said at Holy Communion. It is slightly longer than the Apostles' Creed. It owes its name to the fact that it includes certain clauses about the divine-human person of Jesus Christ which were agreed at the Council of Nicea in AD 325.

Thirdly, there is *the Creed of St. Athanasius*, which is also called *Quicunque Vult* from its opening words 'Whosoever will' (be saved). Although it is not found in the Alternative Service Book, it comes in the Prayer Book just after Morning and Evening Prayer. Nowadays it is hardly ever used, although formerly it took the place of the Apostles' Creed at Morning Prayer on the Great Festivals and certain Saints' Days. It was not written by Athanasius, who was Bishop of Alexandria at the beginning of the fourth century AD, but is called after him because it emphasizes the full divinity of each

Since the creation of the world God's qualities have been seen.

Person of the Trinity just as he did in his great controversy with the presbyter Arius, who denied the essential deity of Jesus. It probably dates from the fifth century AD.

The existence of God

Like the Bible, the creeds assume the existence of God and do not argue it. Ultimately, we accept God's existence by faith rather than by proof because, being infinite, and therefore beyond the reach of our finite minds, God can be known only by his revelation and not by our reason. I do not mean by this that belief in the existence of God is unreasonable. On the contrary, there are sound reasons for believing that he exists. There is no space here to elaborate the five classical arguments for the existence of God which were expounded by Thomas Aquinas. Instead, all I can do is to suggest three lines of thought:

1. The fact of the universe
All round us are phenomena which are inexplicable apart from God. It is reasonable to suppose that just as every building has its

architect, every painting its artist and every mechanism its designer, so the universe, mysterious, beautiful and intricate, must have had its Creator. He is the Cause from which all effects ultimately derive. He is the Life to which all life owes its being. He is the Energy from which all motion comes. These thoughts are expressed by the biblical writers in various ways. 'The heavens declare the glory of God; the skies proclaim the work of his hands' (Psalm 19:1). 'Since the creation of the world God's invisible qualities – his eternal power and divine nature – have been clearly seen, being understood from what has been made' (Romans 1:20). Again, 'the living God, who made heaven and earth and sea and everything in them, ... has not left himself without testimony: he has shown kindness by giving you rain from heaven and crops in their seasons; he provides you with plenty of food and fills your hearts with joy' (Acts 14:15–17).

Following the destruction of the medieval St Paul's Cathedral in the Great Fire of London (1666), Sir Christopher Wren began to design and build the new one which remains. Visitors are often surprised that it contains no memorial to him. His tomb is in the crypt, however, near those of Nelson and Wellington, and above it a plaque bears the Latin inscription *si monumentum requiris, circumspice* ('if you seek his monument, look around you'). Similarly, the world God has made is his best witness.

2. The nature of human beings

If, having looked out at the universe, we now look in at ourselves, we find further evidence for the existence of God. High ideals and lofty aspirations stir within us. Things beautiful to our eyes, ears and touch deeply move us. Our mind is insatiably curious in its quest for knowledge. An imperious urge to do what we 'ought' to do pulls us onward and upward, and burdens us with shame when we fail. Love too discloses the unique nobility of our humanness, the love which has inspired the greatest exploits of art, heroism, sacrifice and service.

Are these universal feelings an empty mockery, a mirage in the desert of illusion? Or is there some ultimate Beauty, Truth, Goodness and Love to which our whole personality responds? More important still: what can be said of our inborn reverence for high and holy things, our sense of awe and wonder, our craze to worship? Why are all human beings worshipping creatures, who manufacture their own gods if none is revealed to them? Is there no God in whose service these longings can find their fulfilment? In the light of these facts of our own experience, it seems more reasonable to believe in God than to deny him.

3. The person of Jesus

If God is infinite, he is beyond us. If he is beyond us, we cannot know him unless he chooses to make himself known. If he were to make himself known, he would surely do so in the highest terms which would be intelligible to us, namely through human personality. It is exactly this that Christians believe he has done. God has not been content to reveal himself only in the universe he has made and in the nature he has given us. He has come himself into our world. In Jesus Christ God became a human being without ceasing to be God. This unique God-man lived on earth, and was seen, heard and touched. The evidence for the deity of Jesus I must leave until the next chapter. It is enough here to say that the best and strongest argument for the existence of God is the Jesus of history. If by chance you are yourself doubtful about God, I urge you to read the Gospels on your knees. 'Seek and you will find,' Jesus said (Matthew 7:7). Come to the historical records of him who claimed to be the Son of the Father, with the open, humble, unprejudiced mind of a little child. It is to people like this, Jesus promised, that God reveals himself (Matthew 11:25).

The Triune God

The Apostles' Creed and the Nicene Creed are divided into three paragraphs which relate to the three Persons of the Trinity. The Alternative Service Book Baptism and Confirmation Services contain a concise summary in the form of questions to the candidates:

> **Do you believe and trust in God the Father
> who made the world?**
>
> **Do you believe and trust in his Son Jesus Christ,
> who redeemed mankind?**
>
> **Do you believe and trust in his Holy Spirit,
> who gives life to the people of God?**

Without doubt, the Trinity is the greatest mystery of the Christian faith. The word itself is a contraction of the words 'tri' and 'unity' and refers to the fact that God is both three and one. To quote from the first of the Thirty-Nine Articles: 'In unity of this Godhead there be three Persons, of one substance, power and eternity, the Father, the Son and the Holy Ghost.'

Some thinkers have been so completely baffled by this concept that they have descended to ridicule. Thomas Jefferson, for example, the third President of the United States, and an eccentric genius, attempted to reconstruct Christianity without any dogmas. He looked forward to the day, he wrote, 'when we shall have done away with the incomprehensible jargon of the Trinitarian arithmetic, that three are one, and one is three'. And one of the most vivid and embarrassing memories of my own school days is of a conversation I had with a visiting clergyman. I was about 15. With the invincible assurance of teenage omniscience I said to him, 'Nobody believes in the Trinity nowadays'. I had no sooner said it than I was ashamed of it. The fact is that I had never thought about the Trinity. Finding it difficult to understand, I jumped to the conclusion that it was an outmoded superstition which intelligent people had long ago discarded. It is perhaps an example of the irony of God's providence that on leaving school I went to that college of Cambridge University which is dedicated to the Holy Trinity!

Our Trinitarian faith

It is true that the word 'Trinity' does not occur in the Bible, and that the doctrine was not clearly formulated by the church fathers until the third and fourth centuries. Nevertheless, the New Testament is Trinitarian through and through. Think how Jesus, when he was baptized to inaugurate his public ministry, heard the Father's voice and saw the Spirit descending on him like a dove, and how at the end, after his resurrection, he commissioned his church to make disciples and baptize them into the name (singular) of the Father, the Son and the Holy Spirit (Matthew 3:16, 17; 28:19). Consider too Peter's statement that we have been 'chosen according to the foreknowledge of God the Father, through the sanctifying work of the Spirit, for obedience to Jesus Christ and sprinkling by his blood' (1 Peter 1:2), and Paul's prayer that 'the grace of the Lord Jesus Christ, and the love of God, and the fellowship of the Holy Spirit'

The River Jordan, in which Jesus was baptized.

might be with us all (2 Corinthians 13:14).

There are three possible approaches to the truth of the Trinity – history, theology and experience – which together constitute a solid foundation for our Trinitarian faith.

History

First, there is the approach of *history*. That is, the doctrine of the Trinity was not invented by unpractical theologians in ivory towers, who had nothing better to do than to speculate. On the contrary, it was a gradually unfolding historical revelation. It happened like this. The apostles were all Jews, who had been brought up to believe in one God (over against the surrounding polytheism), who was both the creator of the world and the covenant God of Israel. Then they met Jesus. As they spent time in his presence, listened to him and watched him, they became convinced that he was the Messiah, yes and more than the Messiah, for he forgave people's sins and even claimed to be the judge of the world. Instinctively, they knew that he was worthy of their worship, in other words that he was God. Yet he was not the Father, because he spoke about the Father and prayed to the Father. Then he began to tell them of somebody else, whom he called either 'the Comforter' or 'the Spirit of truth', who would take his place after he had left them, and who in fact did come on the Day of Pentecost with the fulness of divine grace and power. So it was the facts of their own observation which compelled them to believe in the Trinity. These historical events and experiences left them no alternative.

Theology

Secondly, there is the approach of *theology*. The major problem felt by the early church fathers was how they could reconcile the unity of God with both the deity and the distinctness of Jesus, or how they could believe that Jesus was both divine and distinct from the Father without committing themselves to two Gods All of them began with the unity of God. 'The Lord our God, the Lord is one', they affirmed (Deuteronomy 6:4). Their monotheism was never in question. But then they divided. Some went on to affirm the deity of Jesus. But if God is one and Jesus is divine, and we cannot have two Gods, therefore Jesus cannot have been distinct from the Father. He must have been the same person as the Father, revealing himself in a different mode, so that God was first the Father, then the Son, and then the Holy Spirit. These were the Sabellians (following Sabellius, a third century presbyter from Rome). Their mistake was to deny that Jesus and the Spirit were eternally distinct from the Father.

Others followed a different course. They concluded that, if God is one and Jesus is eternally distinct from the Father, since we cannot have two Gods, therefore Jesus cannot have been fully divine. He must have been a very superior created being, but not God. These were the Arians (following Arius, an early fourth century presbyter in Alexandria). Their mistake was to deny that Jesus was divine.

The fathers' problem, then, was how to affirm that Jesus was both divine and distinct, without contradicting the unity of God. Professor Leonard Hodgson in his book *The Doctrine of the Trinity* (1943) traced the fathers' confusion to their failure to define the nature of God's unity. For there are two kinds of unity – 'mathematical' (which is simple and indivisible) and 'organic' (which is highly complex and may have many component parts). For example, when the atom was discovered, scientists at first thought they had reached the basic unit of matter, only to discover that each atom is itself a tiny universe. Similarly, the unity of God is not mathematical but organic. Within the complex mystery of the infinite God are three eternally distinct personal modes of being, the Father, the Son and the Holy Spirit.

Experience

Thirdly, there is the approach of *experience*. There are many things in life which we cannot fully explain, but nevertheless experience. One might mention electricity, or changes in barometric pressure, or love. Similarly, although we cannot explain the Trinity, yet every time we pray we enjoy access to the Father through the Son by the Spirit (Ephesians 2:18). More particularly, every time we say the Lord's Prayer, perhaps without realising it, we affirm by our three petitions that God is three in One. For it is our heavenly Father who gives us our daily bread, it is through Jesus Christ who died for our sins that we can be forgiven, and it is by the inward power of the Holy Spirit that we can overcome temptation and be rescued from evil. So let no-one say that the Trinity is irrelevant to daily living!

Creator, Ruler and Father

The Apostles' Creed describes God as 'the Father almighty, Creator of heaven and earth'. Here are three statements about God which we must briefly consider.

1. The Creator

The Nicene Creed adds that God is the 'Maker ... of all that is, seen and unseen'. This is a true summary of what the Bible teaches. 'In the beginning God created the heavens and the earth' (Genesis 1:1); '... the LORD made the heavens and the earth, the sea, and all that is in them' (Exodus 20:11); 'there is but one God, the Father, from whom all things came' (1 Corinthians 8:6). We note that in all these verses it is the *fact* of divine creation which is taught, and not the *mode*. The Bible tells us plainly that God is the Creator of all things; it nowhere tells us how he did it, except that everything came into being by his will (Revelation 4:11) as expressed in his word (Genesis 1:3; Psalms 33: 6, 9; Hebrews 11:3). Many Christians today hold some form of the theory of evolution as an expression of God's creative activity, although it is clearly impossible for a biblical Christian to hold a purely *mechanistic* view of the origin and development of life which virtually dispenses with God.

Nor can we regard human beings as nothing but highly evolved animals, for Genesis 1 and 2 affirm the special creation of Adam and Eve in God's image, that is, with a cluster of distinctive faculties (e.g.

reason, conscience, will and love) which make us like God and unlike the animals. Our own self-consciousness strongly confirms this biblical truth. Other Christians want to extend the concept of 'special creation' to everything God has made and to interpret the six days literally. But probably most of us (not least because of the deliberately stylized literary form of Genesis 1) regard the days as representing stages of creation, and would not want to press other details with wooden literalism.

Much of the controversy about the first chapters of Genesis, and indeed of the debate between science and religion in general, has been unnecessary. We Christians have ourselves been open to blame by forgetting that the Bible was not designed by God to be a scientific textbook. I do not mean by this that the biblical and the scientific accounts of things are necessarily incompatible, but rather that they are complementary to one another, and not identical. Their purposes are different. Science addresses itself to 'how' things function; Scripture is preoccupied with 'why' questions.

God's word is designed to make us Christians, not scientists, and to lead us to eternal life through faith in Jesus Christ. It was not God's intention to reveal in Scripture what human beings could discover by their own investigations and experiments. So the first three chapters of Genesis reveal in particular four spiritual truths which could never be discovered by the scientific method. First, that God made everything. Secondly, that he made it out of nothing. There was no original raw material as eternal as himself on which he could work. Thirdly, that he made man male and female in his own image. Fourthly, that everything which he made was 'very good'. When it left his hand it was perfect. Sin and suffering were foreign invasions into his lovely world, and spoiled it.

2. The Sustainer

When the Creed speaks of 'God the Father Almighty', it is referring not so much to his omnipotence as to his control over what he has made. What he created, he sustains. He is 'the Maker and Preserver of all things both visible and invisible' (Article I). God did not wind up the universe like some gigantic clockwork toy and leave it to run on its own. He did not just blow a whistle for the game to begin and then retire to the touchline to watch. No. God is 'immanent' in his universe. That is, he is present and active in it, continually upholding, animating and ordering it and its creatures. Perhaps the dominant theme of the whole Bible is the sovereign, ceaseless, purposeful activity of Almighty God. In contrast to the idols, which had eyes, ears, mouths and hands but could neither see nor hear, neither speak nor act, our God is a living and a busy God.

In its own dramatic and figurative way the Bible leaves us in no doubt of this. The breath of all living creatures is in his hand. The thunder is his voice and the lightning his fire. He causes the sun to shine and the rain to fall. He feeds the birds of the air and clothes the lilies of the field. He makes the clouds his chariot and the winds his messengers. He causes the grass to grow. His trees are well watered. He calms the raging of the sea. He also guides the affairs of people and nations. The mighty empires of Assyria and Babylonia, of Egypt and Persia, of Greece and Rome, were under his overruling control. He called Abraham from Ur. He delivered the Israelites from Egypt, led them across the desert and settled them in the Promised Land. He gave them judges and kings, priests and prophets. Finally he sent his only Son into the world to live, to teach, to die and to rise again.

The Colosseum, Rome, reminder of a mighty empire.

Through him he established his kingdom in the lives of his people. It challenges the old order with its radical values and it will spread worldwide before Christ returns and history ends.

3. The Father

The Creed faithfully reflects the Bible in holding together the majesty and the mercy of God, his greatness and his goodness. It affirms that the Creator of all things condescends to be the Father of those who trust in Jesus Christ. Already in the Old Testament God was known as the Father of Israel, but when Jesus came, the title became more personal and more intimate. He himself used it in addressing, or referring to, God. At the age of twelve he spoke of the temple as his Father's house (Luke 2:49), and his last word on the cross was to commit his spirit into his Father's hands (Luke 23:46). Not only did he himself use this name for God, but he gave us permission to do the same (Matthew 6:9; Luke 11:2). 'Father', then, is Christianity's distinctive title for God. Professor Joachim Jeremias has shown that 'nowhere in the literature of the prayers of ancient Judaism – an immense treasure all too little explored – is this invocation of God as *Abba* to be found .... Jesus on the other hand always used it when he prayed.'[1] Similarly, Muslims have ninety-nine names and titles for Allah (Creator, Sustainer, Provider, Ruler etc.), but not one of them is Father. Perhaps God means it to be his one hundredth name.

God is not, however, the Father of all men and women indiscriminately. Certainly he is the Creator of all. All human beings are his 'offspring' (Acts 17:28) in the sense that they are his creatures. But the title 'Father' was one which Jesus taught specially to his disciples, and both Paul and John make it clear that it is only through the eternal Son of God that we can ourselves become sons and daughters of God in his family. 'To all who received him (Jesus), to those who believed in his name, he gave the right to become children of God' (John 1:12), 'for you are all sons of God through faith in Christ Jesus' (Galatians 3:26).

The universal fatherhood of God and the universal brotherhood of man, of which we hear much, is potential, not actual. It cannot come into being until all men and women submit to Jesus Christ and are born again.

It would be hard to exaggerate the immense privileges we have as members of the family of God. 'How great is the love the Father has lavished on us, that we should be called children of God! And that is what we are!' (1 John 3:1). Only now can we really pray, because only now are we in relationship to God as our Father. He also gives us peace as we trust in him. For with such a Father, how can we be afraid? 'Do not worry,' Jesus used to say – about your life, about your food and clothing, about tomorrow. 'Your heavenly Father knows' was his antidote to anxiety (Matthew 6:25–34, cf v. 8). So it is our duty as well as our privilege to trust God. The children of God have no business to flap or to sulk. Doubt and discontent are unbecoming in us. We must learn both to trust and obey this Father of infinite love, wisdom and power.

Perhaps 'dependence' is the word with which we should leave this chapter. Since God is our Maker and Sustainer, we depend upon him as his creatures. If he is also our heavenly Father, we depend upon him as his children. We have two good reasons to look to him with humble confidence. It is an honour to be the dependants of such a God.

---

[1] *The Central Message of the New Testament* (SCM, 1965), pp. 19–20.

Study guide to chapter 4
See general hints on p. 7

Basic

Questions
1. How would you answer someone who tells you they don't believe in God?
2. How would you answer a Christian who tells you they don't understand the Trinity?
3. Analyse a typical day. How far do you depend on God, and how far on other things? Are you happy with this balance, or would you like to change it in any way?

Creed
Rather than learn a Bible promise on this occasion, learn the Apostle's Creed or any similar statement of faith that your church uses in its services. Ask a church leader for a copy if you have not got one of your own.

Prayer
No 8 on p. 159 – for a steadfast faith in the Trinity.

Extras

Bible study
Psalm 103

In a group
Each describe a 'father-figure' in your life (not necessarily your biological father, but someone you have looked up to and found helpful). In what ways does he (or perhaps she) remind you of God?

Response
Write your own letter to God. Begin it 'Dear Dad (or Father if you find that more natural)' and tell him exactly what is on your heart and mind at the moment. We are often more thorough and more direct in writing than in a silent prayer. You could keep the letter as a reminder for yourself; or you could give it to God in a 'burnt offering' by setting fire to it.

Check-up
Do you find it natural to think of God, and talk to him, as your Father?

Suggestions for further reading
Bruce Milne, *Know the Truth* (IVP, 1982). A handbook of Christian doctrines.
The Trinity
Stuart Olyott, *The Three are One* (Evangelical Press, 1980). A helpful discussion of one of the most difficult Christian concepts.
Alister McGrath, *Understanding the Trinity* (Kingsway, 1990). A more detailed discussion of this doctrine.
Belief in God the Father
J.I. Packer, *Knowing God* (Hodder & Stoughton, 1973). A classic study of the nature and character of God.
Thomas Smail, *The Forgotten Father* (Hodder & Stoughton, 1987). A practical theology of the fatherhood of God.
Tim Hawthorne, *Windows on Science and Faith* (IVP, 1986). How the two can be reconciled when rightly understood.

5. Belief in Jesus Christ

If the first paragraph of the Creed speaks of God the Father, the second speaks of God the Son. It is longer than the other two paragraphs. But this will not surprise us when we remember that the major debates of the early church related to the person of Jesus Christ, and that fundamentally Christianity is Christ. The Creed tells us both who he is and what he came into the world to do. That is, it describes his divine-human person and his saving work.

The person of Christ, or who he is

'I believe ... in Jesus Christ his only Son our Lord ... born of the Virgin Mary.' This concise statement indicates that Jesus of Nazareth was both human, the son of Mary, and divine, the Son of God.

1. The humanity of Jesus

The gospels make it plain that the carpenter-prophet from Nazareth of Galilee was truly human. He was born of a human mother and developed through adolescence to adulthood as all of us do. He had a human body, which felt the pangs of hunger and thirst. The strain of his ceaseless ministry fatigued him. He sat by the well-side to rest and fell asleep on a cushion in the boat. So gruelling was his agony in the garden of Gethsemane that the sweat which fell from him looked like drops of blood. Finally, crucifixion killed him. His dead body was lifted down from the cross, wrapped in grave clothes and laid in a rock tomb.

Jesus had human emotions as well. When he looked at the rich young ruler, he loved him. He burst into tears at the tomb of Lazarus, and wept again over the impenitence of Jerusalem. He also spoke of his joy, which he wanted his disciples to share. He felt compassion both for individuals in pain and for the leaderless crowds, and turned on the Pharisees with anger because of their stubbornness. In addition to his human body and emotions, he had a human spirit. He maintained a close fellowship with his heavenly Father, and regularly sought the solitude of the hills in order to pray. The evidence for his complete humanness is conclusive. Without doubt he was 'the man Christ Jesus' (1 Timothy 2:5).

2. The Virgin Birth of Jesus

The Creed also indicates the origins of the humanity of Jesus, namely that 'he was conceived by the power of the Holy Spirit and born of the Virgin Mary'. In the contemporary debate about the virgin birth, three main questions are commonly asked. First, *what does it mean?* The 'virgin birth' is an unfortunate expression because it lays emphasis on the word 'birth'. But the birth of Jesus was entirely normal and natural. What was abnormal and supernatural was his conception by the Holy Spirit, while his mother Mary remained a virgin.

Secondly, *did it happen?* Matthew and Luke both provide a sober record of this miraculous event. If we give our careful and unbiassed attention to their narrative, I think we will conclude that they were intending to write history not myth (Luke specially claims this in his preface); that their approach is modest and reticent, in contrast to the crudities of pagan stories; and that their accounts are independent of, and complementary to, one another, Matthew telling Joseph's story and Luke Mary's.[1] It is true that Mark and John do not record the virgin birth, but that does not prove they did not know about it. They chose to begin their story with John the Baptist, and made no reference at all to Jesus' birth or boyhood. Are we to deduce from this that they thought he had had neither? Both John and Paul imply the pre-existence of Jesus when they write that 'God sent forth his Son', or that he 'came from above' and 'came into the world'. The likelihood is that they believed this happened through the virgin birth.

Thirdly, *does it matter?* It is a fact that the great New Testament statements of the gospel, which proclaim the death and resurrection of Jesus, do not allude to his virgin birth. The apostles did not use the virgin birth to prove the deity of Jesus. Nor should we. It is better to argue the other way round that if Jesus was the Son of God it was appropriate for him to enter the world by the virgin birth as it was for him to leave it by the ascension. Luke records the angelic announcement to Mary in these words: 'The Holy Spirit will come upon you, and the power of the Most High will overshadow you. So the holy one to be born will be called the Son of God' (Luke 1:35). This verse refers to both the conception and the birth of Jesus. His humanity is traced to the human mother who bore him, his sinlessness and deity to the Holy Spirit who overshadowed her.

3. The deity of Jesus
The Apostles' Creed refers to Jesus not only as Mary's son but as God's, in fact 'his only Son, our Lord'. The Nicene Creed is fuller and describes him as 'the only Son of God, eternally begotten of the Father, God from God, Light from Light, true God from true God, begotten, not made, of one Being with the Father'. The Athanasian Creed clarifies this truth further by affirming that Jesus was 'not made, nor created, but begotten'. These distinctions are important. People 'make' things out of materials (e.g. wood, metals or textiles), 'create' things out of nothing (e.g. an idea, a poem or a tune), but can 'beget' children only out of themselves. So the Son is said to be 'eternally begotten of the Father' or 'God from God', and therefore 'of one Being with the Father'. It is he who 'became incarnate of the Virgin Mary, and was made man' (Nicene Creed), so that he was and still is both God and man simultaneously.

But is this not a pious myth, the fabrication of his over-credulous disciples? No, the cumulative evidence for the deity of Jesus is much stronger than is often realised. Take the gospels as ordinary historical documents, leaving aside the question of their possible inspiration. They portray a peasant carpenter from a humble home in an obscure village, who advanced such claims for himself that we are tempted to question his sanity. His teaching was extraordinarily self-centred. He called God 'the Father' and himself 'the Son' in absolute terms, indicating that there existed between them a unique relationship. He dared to say that he was inaugurating the long-expected kingdom of God, and that people could enter it only by responding to him. He referred to himself neither as a prophet, nor as the greatest of the prophets, but as being himself the fulfilment of all prophecy, since the Scriptures (he said) bore witness to him. He called himself the light of the world and the only way to the Father. He invited people to come to him, promising that he would refresh the thirsty and give the weary rest. He presumed to forgive people's sins (which only God can do), and so incurred the terrible charge of blasphemy. And he shocked his hearers by stating that he would return at the end of history in order to judge the world.

How are we to explain these extravagant claims, which he made with such quiet and unassuming assurance? He was only a young man of barely thirty. He had had very little formal education. He had never travelled outside Palestine. Yet repeatedly, confidently, unostentatiously he advanced his stupendous claims.

Was he mad? a megalomaniac? Was he suffering from a fixed delusion about himself? This suggestion has occasionally been made, but cannot be substantiated. He showed no signs of fanaticism, let alone psychosis. Besides, deluded people delude nobody but themselves, whereas Jesus has convinced millions. The reason is that there was no inconsistency between his claims and his character. On the contrary, he seemed to be who he claimed to be. Take his modesty. Deluded people are obsessed with themselves. If they think they are important, they behave like it. But it is just here that Jesus confounds his critics. Believing himself to be somebody, he acted as if he was nobody. Calling himself the Son of God, he yet put on a slave's apron and washed the apostles' feet. Their lord became their servant. In addition he made friends with the outcasts of society, welcomed prostitutes and touched untouchables. He gave himself in selfless service to others. And then he surrendered to unjust arrest, trial and condemnation. He made no attempt to resist when he was mocked, flogged, spat on and crucified. He even prayed for the forgiveness of his tormentors.

All this evidence adds up to an extraordinary paradox. Jesus was extremely self-centred in his words, but absolutely unself-centred in his deeds. He sounded proud, but he was humble. In his teaching he advanced himself; in his ministry he forgot himself in the will of his Father and the welfare of people. This combination of egocentricity and humility has no parallel in the history of the world. The only way to resolve it is to acknowledge that Jesus of Nazareth was and is the Son of God.

Add to this paradox the Resurrection, and the case is complete. No satisfactory explanation has ever been given of the disappear-

The 'Tomb of the Herods', Jerusalem.

ance of Jesus' body from the tomb except that God raised him from the dead. We also have to put alongside the disappearance of the body the reappearance of the Lord. The apostles insisted that they saw him, several times and in several places. They were tough fishermen; they were not liable to hallucinations. Rather the reverse. They refused at first to believe the story; but their scepticism was overcome. And their subsequent actions corroborated their change of mind. They were transformed people. No longer disillusioned or intimidated, they came out of hiding, confronted the Jewish authorities, and boldly proclaimed Jesus and the resurrection. They were willing to risk imprisonment and death. Nothing can adequately account for these things except that he had indeed been raised from death.

So he was the Son of God, as he was also the son of Mary. The historical evidence for both his humanity and his deity is compelling. Moreover the Creeds wisely affirm these two truths about him without attempting to reconcile them. 'Our Lord Jesus Christ, the Son of God', says the Athanasian Creed, 'is God and Man; God, of the substance of the Father, begotten before the worlds; and Man, of the substance of his mother, born in the world, Perfect God and Perfect Man.' In consequence, quoting now the second of the Thirty-nine Articles, 'two whole and perfect natures, that is to say, the Godhead and Manhood, were joined together in One Person, never to be divided, whereof is one Christ, very God and very Man.'

The work of Christ, or what he did

1. The death of Jesus

The Creeds pass straight from the birth of Jesus to his death, from the mother who bore him to the judge who condemned him: 'he was ... born of the Virgin Mary. He suffered under Pontius Pilate, was crucified, died, and was buried.' The reference to Pilate reminds us that the crucifixion was a historical event, for he was a notorious procurator of the Roman province of Judea, an efficient but ruthless administrator. Further, the immediate leap from the birth to the death of Jesus indicates its centrality. It is scarcely an exaggeration to say that he was born in order to die. He kept predicting his death as inevitable[2] and referring to it as the 'hour' for which he had come into the world (e.g. John 12:27). When on his last evening he instituted a supper to commemorate him, the bread and wine he gave them spoke of neither his birth nor his life, neither his teaching nor his miracles, but of his violent death on the cross. It was above all for this that he wished to be remembered. All his apostles came to understand that his death was 'of first importance' (1 Corinthians 15:3), and Paul added that he would boast in nothing else and preach nothing else (Galatians 6:14; 1 Corinthians 2:2). It is therefore not an accident that the symbol of Christianity is a cross.

Then why did he die? The Creeds do not tell us, but the New Testament does. In fact it lists several reasons. He died as a martyr to his own greatness, the victim of small minds and evil hearts (e.g. Acts 2:23; 3:13–15; 4:27). He died to set an example of how to bear unjust suffering without retaliation (e.g. 1 Peter 2:21–23). He died to reveal the inexhaustible and inextinguishable love of God (e.g. Romans 5:8; 1 John 4:10). He also died as our representative, so that as he died and rose again, we should ourselves die to sin and live for righteousness (e.g. 1 Peter 2:24). So he died as a martyr, an example, a revelation and a representative. We must not forget these. But above all he died as a Saviour. It was 'for us men and for our salvation' that he 'came down from heaven' (Nicene Creed) and laid down his life. Indeed, the apostles regularly say that 'he died for our sins'. What they implied by this should be clear from the fact that the Bible from beginning to end links death to sin as its just reward. 'The wages of sin is death' (Romans 6:23). If, then, *he died* for *our* sins, it must mean that he bore in our place the penalty which our sins had deserved.

Consider two statements of the apostle Peter's. The first is that 'he himself bore our sins in his body on the tree' (1 Peter 2:24). Since throughout the Old Testament to 'bear sin' means to 'bear the penalty of sin', this assertion is self-explanatory. The second statement is that 'Christ died for sins once for all, the righteous for the unrighteous, to bring you to God' (1 Peter 3:18). Here it is plain that Christ's goal was to reconcile us to God, while the means was his death, the innocent in place of the guilty, in order to put away the sins which had previously separated us from him. The awful God-forsaken darkness which Jesus endured on the cross was the very hell which our sins deserve.

> *We may not know, we cannot tell*
> *what pains he had to bear,*
> *but we believe it was for us*
> *he hung and suffered there.*
>
> *He died that we might be forgiven,*
> *he died to make us good;*
> *that we might go at last to heaven,*
> *saved by his precious blood.*
>
> *There was no other good enough*
> *to pay the price of sin;*
> *he only could unlock the gate*
> *of heaven – and let us in.*

Only because the sinless Son of God was 'made sin for us' and 'made a curse for us', to quote two of Paul's most startling statements (2 Corinthians 5:21; Galatians 3:13), can we sinners be forgiven. In and through the death of his Son, God has himself borne the condemnation of our sins, becoming simultaneously the judge and the judged, and so perfectly satisfying both his justice and his love, in order to offer us a free forgiveness. No wonder the Apostles' Creed ends with a reference to 'the forgiveness of sins, the resurrection of the body and the life everlasting', for these are 'the benefits of his passion', the blessings Christ has won for us by his death. We shall sing with the angels throughout eternity: 'Worthy is the Lamb, who was slain, to receive power and wealth and wisdom and strength and honour and glory and praise!' (Revelation 5:12).

But the Creed does not end with Christ on his cross. It goes on to mention in rapid succession five other events of his saving career.

2. The descent, resurrection and ascension of Jesus

First, 'he descended into hell'. This has puzzled generations of believers, because they have thought that 'hell' means 'gehenna', the place of punishment. But the old Anglo-Saxon word 'hell' translated rather the Greek *hadēs*, meaning simply 'the place of departed spirits' or 'the abode of the dead'. This is why 'death and hades' are often bracketed in the New Testament (e.g. Revelation 1:18; 20:13, 14), as the event and the place to which it leads. Modern versions of the Creed tend to render the statement 'he descended to the dead'. The reason why the clause was included in the Creed is to show that Jesus, after the death and burial of his body, went in his spirit to the next world (until his resurrection on Easter Day). He went there partly to announce the great victory he had won on the cross, and partly to assure us that he had now been through all experiences which are integral to our humanity, including death and hades, which should therefore hold no fears for us.

Secondly, 'on the third day he rose again'. As the clause 'suffered under Pontius Pilate' witnesses to the historicity of Jesus' death, so the clause 'on the third day' witnesses to the historicity of his resurrection. It was a definite and datable event. The soul and body of Jesus, which had been sundered at his death (his body remaining in the tomb, his soul going to *hadēs*), were now reunited and he was gloriously changed. It became evident that there were both continuity and discontinuity between his earthly and his resurrection bodies. His new body was the same as the old (his appearance, scars and voice were recognized), and yet wonderfully different from it (possessing new powers, appearing and disappearing, materializing and passing through closed doors). We should insist, against the denials by one or two church leaders, that 'resurrection' means 'bodily resurrection' (1) because of the evangelists' witness that the tomb was empty, (2) because the apostolic tradition affirmed that Jesus 'died, was buried, was raised and was seen' (1 Corinthians 15:3–5), so that what was raised was what had been buried, i.e. his body, and (3) because the resurrected body of Jesus was and is the first bit of the material universe which has been redeemed, and is

The Mount of Olives, from which the risen Christ ascended.

therefore the beginning and the pledge of God's new creation.

Thirdly, 'he ascended into heaven'. There is no need for us to be embarrassed by the story of the Ascension. Luke certainly believed it was a historical event, for he emphasized that it happened before eye-witnesses (Acts 1:9–11). Nor should we be shifted from our ground by the ridicule of people who think it funny to present the Ascension as a 'lift-off' and Jesus as the first cosmonaut. For Jesus could easily have 'gone to the Father' invisibly and secretly. He had after all disappeared several times during the forty days between the Resurrection and the Ascension. The reason why he went visibly and publicly was to convince his apostles that he had gone for good. They must now wait, not for him to re-appear, but for the Holy Spirit to come.

3. The session and return of Jesus

Fourthly, 'he ... is seated at the right hand of the Father'. This is as clearly and surely a metaphorical assertion as the references to Jesus' death, descent, resurrection and ascension were historical. Nor is the metaphor hard to interpret. When King Solomon gave his mother an audience, 'he had a throne brought for the king's mother, and she sat down at his right hand' (1 Kings 2:19). In virtually every culture to be seated at the right hand is to be given the place of honour. Additionally, as we have seen earlier, Jesus is 'seated' there because he is resting from his finished work of redemption. The priests stood in the temple, and no seats were provided for them, because their sacrificial labours were never done. Day after day, week after week, month after month, and year after year they offered 'the same sacrifices, which can never take away sins'. 'But when this priest (Jesus) had offered for all time one sacrifice for sins, he sat down at the right hand of God' (Hebrews 10:11, 12). Now he waits until his victory is universally acknowledged and his enemies are made his footstool (Psalms 110:1).

Fifthly, 'he will come again to judge the living and the dead'. The reason we believe that Jesus Christ is coming back is that he said so (e.g. Mark 14:62). Some people maintain that he expected his *parousia* ('coming') to take place within the lifetime of his contemporaries, and that he was mistaken. But since he confessed that he did not himself know the date of his return (Mark 13:32), it is extremely unlikely that he would have taught when it would take

Many tombs are clustered around the Mount of Olives.

place. What he surely intended by his urgent predictions was to persuade his followers to 'watch', because they did not know when the
time would come (e.g. Mark 13:33–37). As we look forward to the
Parousia, we should neither 'demythologize' it (denying that it will
be an event of history) nor 'embroider' it (decorating it with our
own speculative fancies). Instead, if we are wise and humble, we will
acknowledge that much remains mysterious, and we will be careful
not to go beyond the plain teaching of Scripture. While refusing to
dogmatize over details, we can then affirm at least that the Lord's
coming will be personal ('this same Jesus', 'the Lord himself' – Acts
1:11; 1 Thessalonians 4:16), visible ('every eye will see him' – Revelation 1:7), universal and undisputed ('like the lightning' – Luke
17:24), and glorious (in 'the majesty of his power' – 2 Thessalonians 1:9). 'He will come again in glory', says the Nicene Creed; his
second coming will be as spectacular as his first was lowly and
obscure.

The main purpose of his coming will be to apply to his people all
the remaining blessings of the salvation he has won for them. He
will raise them from the dead, giving them new and glorious bodies
like his (Philippians 4:21), and he will transfer them to the promised
'new heaven and new earth, the home of righteousness' (2 Peter

3:13). But the Creed focusses on the second purpose of his coming, namely to judge. He claimed that the Father had 'entrusted all judgment to the Son' (John 5:22, 27), and his apostles declared that God had already appointed the judge and fixed the day (Acts 10:42; 17:31). Then those who have refused to repent and believe will suffer the terrible fate of 'eternal destruction and exclusion from the presence of the Lord' (2 Thessalonians 1: 9 RSV), while those who have fled to Jesus for refuge from their sins and from God's wrath will inherit 'his kingdom' which 'will have no end' (Nicene Creed).

---

[1] Some readers are troubled by the way in which Matthew regards the virgin birth as the fulfilment of a prophecy by Isaiah, namely that 'a virgin will be with child and will give birth to a son, and they will call him "Emmanuel", which means "God with us"' (Isaiah 7:14; Matthew 1:23). The problem is that Matthew quotes the LXX version of the prophecy, which contains the Greek word *parthenos* ('virgin'), whereas Isaiah used the Hebrew word *almah* (often translated 'young woman'). This is a well known conundrum. But two points may be made in defence of Matthew. First, Isaiah did not use the common Hebrew word for a married woman or wife (*ishshah*), but a rare one which was sometimes used of an unmarried girl. Perhaps this is why the LXX chose *parthenos* for the Greek translation. Secondly, in quoting Isaiah 7:14, Matthew lays more emphasis on the meaning of the child's name 'Emmanuel' ('God with us') than on the status of the child's mother. These two points permit the conclusion that, although Isaiah 7:14 does not clearly assert the virgin birth, it is compatible with it and an appropriate text for Matthew to have quoted.

[2] e.g. 'the Son of man must suffer ... ' (Mark 8:31).

Study guide to chapter 5
See general hints on p. 7

Basic

Extras

Questions
1. How would you answer someone who says, 'Jesus was obviously a great religious teacher, but I can't believe he was the Son of God'?
2. Some church leaders today say it is not necessary to believe that Jesus' virgin birth, bodily resurrection or ascension really happened. Do you agree or disagree? Why?
3. What is Jesus doing now?

Promise
Christ's abiding presence – Matthew 28:20; Hebrews 13:5, 6.

Prayer
No 8 on p. 159 – for a steadfast faith in the Trinity.

Bible study
Philippians 2:5–11

In a group
Choose and sing some of your favourite hymns or songs about Jesus. What do you particularly like about them?

Response
One of the oldest Christian prayers in the world is 'The Jesus Prayer', based on some words in one of his parables:
Lord Jesus Christ,
Son of God,
Have mercy on me,
A sinner.
Pray it quietly or silently several times, allowing Jesus to call to your mind and forgive any unconfessed sin as you do so.

Check-up
Do you worship Jesus as God in your mind and in your whole life?

Suggestions for further reading
The Person of Christ
R.T. France, *Jesus the Radical* (IVP, 1989). A portrait of Jesus, which shows his significance for today.
Roy Clements, *Introducing Jesus* (Kingsway, 1986). An exposition of the discourses of Jesus in John's Gospel, this book is simply written but probes some deep issues.
Christ's death
John R.W. Stott, *The Cross of Christ* (IVP, 1986). A thorough biblical survey of the meaning and implications of the death of Christ.
Christ's resurrection
Michael Green, *The Empty Cross of Jesus* (Hodder & Stoughton, 1984). The importance of keeping together the death and the resurrection of Jesus.
Christ's return
Stephen H. Travis, *I believe in the Second Coming of Jesus* (Hodder & Stoughton, 1988). The biblical hope and its challenge.

6. Belief in the Holy Spirit

I remember reading some years ago about a man in China who was enquiring about the Christian faith but was very perplexed about the Holy Spirit – the more so after he had read how at Jesus' baptism the Spirit descended on him like a dove. 'The Father I understand', the Chinese enquirer said, 'and Jesus Christ his Son, but who is this holy bird?' One sympathizes with his confusion. And the use of the old English word 'Ghost' (which has not yet been altogether abandoned) has not helped. People then think of the 'Holy Ghost' as a kind of phantom or spectre, and on that account are afraid of him or do not take him seriously.

Another reason why it is difficult to understand the Holy Spirit is that he is a shy, reticent, self-effacing Spirit. Unlike us, he finds no pleasure in drawing attention to himself or being lionized. Too much publicity embarrasses him. Instead, his chief ministry is to bear witness to both the Father and the Son. It is he who causes us in prayer to say 'Abba, Father', and it is he who enables us to confess 'Jesus is Lord' (Romans 8:15; 1 Corinthians 12:3). In fact, his distinctive role has been described as 'a floodlight ministry in relation to the Lord Jesus Christ ... When floodlighting is well done, the floodlights are so placed that you do not see them ...; what you are meant to see is just the building on which the floodlights are trained.' So the Holy Spirit is 'the hidden floodlight shining on the Saviour'.[1]

The first truth about the Holy Spirit which needs to be affirmed is that he is God, the third person of the Trinity. He is therefore eternal. He was also active in creation and shares in its renewal (Genesis 1:2; Psalms 104:30).

As God he is omnipresent, so that the Psalmist asked 'Where can

I go from your Spirit? Where can I flee from your presence?' (Psalm 139:7). To lie to him is to lie to God (Acts 5:3, 4, 9), and defiantly to reject what we know to be true is to blaspheme against him (Mark 3:29). Because he was sent by both the Father and the Son (John 14:16; 16:17), he is called equally 'the Spirit of God' and 'the Spirit of Christ'. More than that, Jesus referred to him as 'proceeding from the Father' (John 15:26), that is, deriving his divine being from him eternally. The Nicene Creed adds that he proceeds also 'from the Son'. This so-called *Filioque* clause was long disputed, and became a major cause of the schism between the Eastern and Western churches in 1054. It certainly lacks clear biblical support. Nevertheless, all agree with the Nicene Creed's statement that the Holy Spirit is 'the Lord' (cf. 2 Corinthians 3:17,18), who 'with the Father and the Son together is worshipped and glorified'. In fact, equal honour is due to each person of the Trinity. The Athanasian Creed states the matter clearly: 'The Godhead of the Father, and of the Son, and of the Holy Spirit, is all one: the Glory equal, the Majesty co-eternal .... So the Father is God, the Son is God, and the Holy Spirit is God. And yet they are not three Gods, but one God.'

The personality of the Holy Spirit

The Holy Spirit, who is God, is also personal. Some Christians find this difficult to grasp because the Holy Spirit never has had or will have a body. But you can be personal without being corporeal. We ourselves, during the interim period between death and resurrection, will be disembodied spirits, but we shall not cease to be personal.

There are two main reasons for believing in the personality of the Holy Spirit. First, in the Greek of John's Gospel Jesus is recorded as referring to the Holy Spirit five times by the emphatic pronoun *ekeinos*, 'he' (John 14:26; 15:26; 16:8,13,14). This is the more striking because the masculine 'he' is in apposition to the neuter noun *pneuma*, 'Spirit'. Thus theology triumphs over grammar! The Holy Spirit is not a vague, indefinable influence, but a living person, not an 'it' but a 'he'.[2]

The second reason is that Jesus and his apostles spoke of the Holy Spirit as having mind, feeling and will, which are commonly recognized as the three constituents of personality. Paul wrote of 'the mind of the Spirit' (Romans 8:27) and referred to him as searching, teaching, testifying and speaking, all of which are impossible without a mind. That the Spirit also has feelings is clear from the command not to 'grieve' him (Ephesians 4:30). This Greek verb occurs forty-two times in the New Testament, and on each occasion refers to persons. Only persons can feel sorrow. The Holy Spirit also has a will, for he distributes gifts to different believers, 'just as he determines' (1 Corinthians 12:11). Since he is able to think, to grieve and to make decisions, we must conclude that he is fully personal.

The work of the Holy Spirit

During his last evening with the Twelve in the upper room Jesus astonished them by saying: 'It is for your good that I am going away. Unless I go away, the Counsellor will not come to you; but if I go, I will send him to you' (John 16:7). In what ways was the ministry of the Spirit better than that of the Son? In two ways. First, the Holy Spirit *universalizes* the presence of Jesus. On earth the disciples could not enjoy uninterrupted fellowship with their Master, for when they were in Galilee, he might be in Jerusalem, or vice versa. His presence was limited to one place at one time. But no longer. Now through his Spirit Jesus is with us everywhere and always. Secondly, the Holy Spirit *internalizes* the presence of Jesus. He said to the disciples: 'You know him (the Spirit of truth, the Counsellor), for he lives with you and will be in you. I will not leave you as orphans; I will come to you' (John 14:17, 18). On earth Jesus was with them and could teach them, but he could not enter their personality and change them from within. Now, however, through the Holy Spirit Christ dwells in our hearts by faith (Ephesians 3:16, 17) and does his transforming work there.

The Holy Spirit has sometimes been called the 'executive' of the Godhead, meaning that what the Father and the Son desire to do in the world and the church today, they execute through the Holy Spirit. The Creeds tell us little about this work, but it is fully described in the documents of the New Testament. We will consider seven areas of his ministry.

1. Christian conversion

The experience of conversion is from first to last the work of the

Holy Spirit. One of his titles is 'the Spirit of grace' (Hebrews 10:29) because, like the Father and the Son, he yearns with undeserved mercy for the salvation of sinners. Without his gracious influence nobody would ever come to Christ.

He begins by 'convicting' (or convincing) the world of 'sin, righteousness and judgment' (John 16:8–10). Every stab of conscience and pang of guilt, every sense of alienation and longing for reconciliation, and every anxious fear of coming judgment are prompted by him. Next, he opens our eyes to see the truth, glory and saving power of Jesus. Indeed, his most characteristic ministry in this age is to bear witness to Jesus Christ (John 15:26). True, we are called to be his witnesses too, but our witness is always secondary. The Holy Spirit is the primary witness, and without his witness ours would be futile. Having shown us our sin and our Saviour, the Holy Spirit moves us to repent and believe, and so to experience the new birth. For to be born again is to be 'born of the Spirit' (John 3:6–8). It is he who gives life to those who were previously dead in their transgressions and sins (Ephesians 2:1–5); the Nicene Creed rightly calls him 'the Lord, the Giver of life'.

2. Christian assurance

The Holy Spirit dwells in those he has regenerated, and his presence within us is God's 'seal' to indicate that we are now his own (2 Corinthians 1:22; Ephesians 1:13; 4:30). Conversely, 'if anyone does not have the Spirit of Christ, he does not belong to Christ' (Romans 8:9). In addition to being an objective token that we belong to God, the indwelling Spirit actively assures us of God's love and fatherhood (Romans 5:5; 8:16). Then there is something more. The Spirit not only seals, and witnesses to, our present privileges; he is also the guarantee of our future inheritance (2 Corinthians 1:22; Ephesians 1:14). The Greek word for 'guarantee' is *arrabōn*, whose equivalent in modern Greek is used for an engagement ring, the pledge of marriage. In first-century Greek, however, it was used commercially of a down payment or deposit. It is as if God, in giving us his Spirit, has handed over to us the first instalment of our salvation, assuring us that the fulness will in due course be ours as well.

These three pictures – the seal (claiming ownership), the witness (giving inner confidence) and the guarantee (pledging the final inheritance) – all illustrate aspects of the Holy Spirit's work in bringing assurance to the people of God.

Perhaps this is the best place for me to say something about the so-called 'baptism of (or with, or in) the Holy Spirit'. The teaching of the pentecostal churches, and of many people in the charismatic or neo-pentecostal movement, is that we receive the 'gift' of the Spirit when we first believe, but then need a second and subsequent experience called the 'baptism' of the Spirit, usually evidenced by 'speaking in tongues'. What the New Testament teaches, however, is not a stereotype of two stages, but rather the initial blessing of regeneration by the Spirit, followed by a process of growth into maturity, during which we may indeed be granted many deeper and richer experiences of God. These often bring a fresh experience of the reality of God and a more vivid awareness of his love. But they should not be called 'the baptism of the Spirit'. The expression to be 'baptized with the Spirit' occurs only seven times in the New Testament. Six of them are quotations of John the Baptist's words 'I baptize with water, but he will baptize with the Spirit', a promise which was fulfilled on the Day of Pentecost. The seventh (1 Corinthians 12:13) emphasizes that all of us have been 'baptized' with the Spirit and been made to 'drink' of the Spirit – two graphic pictures of our having received him.

3. Christian holiness

The Christian life is a holy life because our God is a holy God. It is impossible to read the Bible and miss this. In both Old and New Testaments God challenges his people: 'Be holy, because I am holy'.[3] God the Father, we read, 'chose us ... before the creation of the world to be holy ...' (Ephesians 1:4). The Lord Jesus 'gave himself for us to redeem us from all wickedness and to purify for himself a people that are his very own, eager to do what is good' (Titus 2:14). Moreover, it is because God calls us 'to live a holy life' that he gives us 'his Holy Spirit' (1 Thessalonians 4:7, 8). Each person of the Trinity is thus actively concerned for our holiness.

But it is specially the Holy Spirit, as his name indicates, who is committed to promoting holiness in the people of God. His ministry is not only to show Christ to us, but to form Christ in us. And he does it by penetrating deeply into the hidden recesses of our personality. Teaching, example and exhortation are all important, but they are no substitute for inward power. Only he can control the evil and cultivate the good within us. This does not mean that we have no part in the process, however. In the conflict between 'the flesh' (our fallen human nature) and 'the Spirit' (the indwelling Holy Spirit), which Paul describes, he urges us to take up the right attitude to both. On the one hand, 'those who belong to Christ Jesus have crucified the sinful nature with its passions and desires'. That is, we are to be ruthless in our rejection of everything we know to be wrong (Galatians 5:24). On the other hand, we are to 'live by the Spirit', be 'led by the Spirit' and 'keep in step with the Spirit', surrendering daily to his mastery and following his promptings (Galatians 5:16, 18, 25).

4. Christian understanding

One of Jesus' favourite titles for the Holy Spirit was 'the Spirit of truth' (John 14:17; 15:26; 16:13). It is clear therefore that the Holy Spirit believes, loves, defends and teaches the truth, and that Christians who are filled with the Spirit will share his concerns.

His commitment to the truth is seen first and foremost in his inspiration of the Scriptures. The Nicene Creed includes the significant expression that 'he spoke through the prophets'. I shall have more to say about the Bible in chapter 8. Meanwhile, it is enough to note what the Creed says. The prophets were the vehicles of the Holy Spirit's revelation. He spoke through them in such a way that their words were also truly his words. According to the writer to the Hebrews, 'God spoke through the prophets' (Hebrews 1:1). According to Peter, 'men spoke from God' (2 Peter 1:21). Thus, God spoke and men spoke. Both are true. This is the double authorship of Scripture. We must not affirm either in such a way as to contradict the other. Moreover, what is true of the Old Testament prophets is equally true of the New Testament apostles, whom Jesus 'sent' out to preach and teach, just as God had 'sent' the prophets with his message to Israel. And Jesus promised his apostles the same ministry of the Holy Spirit which the prophets had enjoyed: 'he will teach you all things ... he will guide you into all the truth' (John 15:26; 16:13).

If the Holy Spirit is the primary author of Scripture, he is its primary interpreter too. In fact the history of the church is the story of how the Holy Spirit has led his people (in spite of some sad lapses on their part) into a progressive understanding of the meaning and application of the Bible. And although we need each other's help in the Christian community if we are to be protected against our own culturally limited and distorted interpretations, yet we also have the privilege of reading the Bible by ourselves. This is what the Reformers called 'the right of private judgment'.

At the same time, we need to cry humbly to the Holy Spirit for his illumination. Otherwise, our reading will degenerate into a meaningless routine. I know this from my own experience. For I was brought up to read the Bible daily, but found it a dull and boring duty. After I had opened the door to Christ, however, the Bible began at once to be a new book to me. Not, of course, that I now understood everything. But it spoke to me. That is, God spoke to me through it. It is good and necessary therefore to pray before we read: 'Open my eyes that I may see wonderful things in your law' (Psalm 119:18). Have you ever tried to tell the time from a sundial on a cloudy day? You cannot; it is impossible. All you can see is figures, with no message. But when the sun breaks through and shines on the dial, immediately the finger points and we receive the message. It is just the same with the Scriptures and the Spirit.

5. Christian fellowship

Our grasp of the ministry of the Holy Spirit is often too individualistic. Even in this chapter we have so far concentrated on his work in each Christian's conversion, assurance, holiness and understanding. But now we note that in the Apostles' Creed we say we 'believe in the Holy Spirit, the holy catholic church', because the Holy Spirit is the creator of the church. It is not strictly accurate to say that the church was born on the Day of Pentecost, as some people assert, since the church as the people of God had existed at least from the time of God's covenant with Abraham some 2000 years before Christ. What happened at Pentecost was that the remnant of God's people became the Spirit-filled body of Christ.

The church of Christ is essentially a fellowship, a *koinōnia*, which is a word expressing what we have in common (*koinos*) as the people of God. Indeed, it is essentially the fellowship of the Spirit, because it is our common participation in him which unites us. If he dwells in you and in me, his presence in us has made us one. We may never have met, or even have heard of one another, but the Holy Spirit has united us. 'There is one body and one Spirit', wrote Paul

(Ephesians 4:4). He might have said 'there is one body *because* there is one Spirit', since it is the one Spirit who creates and animates the one body, the body of Christ.

So in one sense the church is not divided and cannot be. Even our outward divisions do not tear it asunder, since the one Spirit indwells it. Piers in a harbour may divide it into sections, so that boats are cut off from each other, but the same sea flows and swells underneath. Our man-made denominations also separate us outwardly and visibly, but inwardly and invisibly the tide of the Spirit unites us. The Nicene Creed characterizes the church as 'one, holy, catholic and apostolic', which are the four classical 'marks' or 'notes' of the church. And they are true. The church is both one and holy because the Holy Spirit has united and sanctified it, setting it apart to belong to God, even though in practice it is often disunited and unholy. The church is also catholic (embracing all believers and all truth) and apostolic (affirming the teaching of the apostles and engaging in mission), even though in practice it often denies the faith it should profess and the mission it should pursue.

At the same time, we must not take refuge in our affirmation that the church is 'one, holy, catholic and apostolic' as an excuse for acquiescing in its disunity, impurity, sectarianism and inactivity. On the contrary, our vision of the ideal should inspire us to seek a closer approximation of the reality to it. In seeking this, we should also remember 'the communion of saints', which the Creed mentions next. It means that the church militant on earth and the church triumphant in heaven, even if they cannot actively commune with one another, are still united by the Spirit, especially when our worship is caught up with theirs.

6. Christian service

The Holy Spirit is concerned not only to unite, but also to 'edify' or build up the church. In order to do so, he gives church members a whole variety of gifts. Paul explains this by elaborating his image of the church as the body of Christ. Just as the human body is one, he writes, but has many members (limbs and organs), each with a different function, just so the body of Christ is one but its members have been endowed with different gifts. It is important to distinguish between the 'gift' of the Spirit (that is, the Holy Spirit himself who has been given to us) and the 'gifts' of the Spirit (that is, the aptitudes which he bestows on believers). The same gift is given to all and brings unity to the church; different gifts are distributed among all, which bring diversity to the church.

Several questions are commonly asked about the Spirit's gifts or *charismata*. First, what are they? There are four lists of them in the New Testament.[4] They add up to about twenty-one. So haphazard are these listings that they seem to be selective rather than exhaustive. Probably there are many more gifts which are not mentioned. Some are supernatural (e.g. miracles – 1 Corinthians 12:10, 28), but others are not and are even quite mundane (e.g. gifts of administration – 1 Corinthians 12:28, giving money and showing mercy – Romans 12:8). Many seem to be natural abilities which are now intensified and Christianized. Secondly, what is their purpose? They are service gifts. Each of the four lists stresses that they are given to be used for the common good, so that the church is built up and grows into maturity.

Thirdly, which are the more important gifts? Since they are given to build up the church, we must evaluate them according to the degree to which they do so. By this criterion it seems to me that we should emphasize the teaching gifts, since nothing nurtures the church like the truth. Whatever our gifts (and the implication is that every member of Christ's body has at least one), we must neither depreciate our gift while being jealous of others', nor despise other people's gifts while boasting of our own (1 Corinthians 12:14–26). We will be spared these follies, and especially any over-emphasis on the more spectacular gifts, if we are filled with that love of Christ in comparison with which all gifts are worth nothing (1 Corinthians 13).

7. Christian mission

The same Holy Spirit who sanctifies, unites and builds up the church is also concerned to evangelize the world. For he is essentially a missionary Spirit. This is clear from Jesus' teaching. He promised one day that 'streams of living water' would flow out from within each believer, and John added that he was referring to the Holy Spirit (John 7:38,39). Archbishop William Temple commented on this verse as follows: 'No-one can possess (or rather be indwelt by) the Spirit of God, and keep that Spirit to himself. Where the Spirit is, he flows forth; if there is no flowing forth, he is not there.'

Witnesses to Christ soon reached Rome.

What Jesus taught in this verse is abundantly illustrated in the Acts, in which we first see the outpouring of the Spirit on the Day of Pentecost and then watch him push his people out as witnesses in ever-widening circles, beginning in Jerusalem, the capital of Jewry, and ending in Rome, the capital of the world. 'The book of the Acts is strictly a missionary book', wrote that notable Anglican missionary Roland Allen. 'The conclusion is irresistible that the Spirit given ... was in fact a missionary Spirit'.[5] This, he goes on, is 'the great, fundamental, unmistakable teaching of the book'.[6] So then we too 'must be missionaries ... unless we are ready to deny the Holy Spirit of Christ as revealed in the Acts'.[7]

Now I do not think Roland Allen meant that all Christians must be cross-cultural 'missionaries' in the technical, professional sense, although to be sure this is a great and honourable calling to some. I think he meant that we are all called to be witnesses to Jesus Christ – at home, at work, among our friends and neighbours – and that for this task the power of the Holy Spirit is indispensable (Acts 1:8). Our local church should be committed to mission too, both local mission as it reaches out to those who live in the parish and global mission as it supports by prayer and money the worldwide evangelistic task of the church.

Many Christians shrink from the responsibility of witness

because we are naturally shy and reserved. But the Holy Spirit can give us courage. He enabled timid, uneducated fishermen to speak boldly for Jesus (Acts 4:13,31). Paul had the same experience. Although he had a powerful intellect, tradition says he was little and ugly, and his critics disparaged him as being unimpressive in both personality and speech (2 Corinthians 10:10). He said of himself that when he first came to Corinth he arrived 'in weakness and fear, and with much trembling' (1 Corinthians 2:3). In consequence, he relied not on eloquence of speech or worldly wisdom but on 'a demonstration of the Spirit's power' (1 Corinthians 2:4). That is to say, the Holy Spirit took his words spoken in human weakness and carried them home with great power to the mind, heart, conscience and will of his hearers.

All this is extremely relevant to the Decade of Evangelism on which, as I write, the Anglican Communion has just embarked. The danger is that we shall rely on the wrong things. Do we want to be faithful witnesses to Jesus Christ? Then we must have his power. Do we want his power? Then we must have his Spirit.

There is perhaps no greater need in the contemporary church than that we should be filled with the Holy Spirit (Ephesians 5:18). We need him not only to bring us to conversion and assurance, nor only to sanctify, enlighten, unite and equip us, but also to reach out through us in blessing to an alienated world, like rivers of living water which irrigate the desert.

---

[1] James I. Packer, *Keep in Step with the Spirit* (IVP, 1984), pp. 65–66.

[2] It is true that AV sometimes uses the expression 'the Spirit itself' (e.g. Romans 8:16, 26). This is because the Greek reflexive pronoun is neuter like the noun 'Spirit'. But RSV and NIV abandon grammatical accuracy for theological correctness and translate 'the Spirit himself'.

[3] e.g. 1 Peter 1:16, quoting Leviticus 11:44, 45; 19:2; 20:7 etc.

[4] Romans 12:3–8; 1 Corinthians 12:4–11, 27–31; Ephesians 4:7–13; and 1 Peter 4:10, 11.

[5] Roland Allen, *Pentecost and the World* (Oxford University Press, 1917), p.36.

[6] ibid., p.40

[7] ibid., p.91.

Study guide to chapter 6
See general hints on p. 7

Basic

Questions
1. How would you answer a new Christian who says, 'I don't understand the Holy Spirit'?
2. How far are you aware of the Holy Spirit working in the areas this chapter outlines (a) in your own life; (b) in your church? How could you help to strengthen any weak areas?

Promise
Helping others – John 7:38, 39.

Prayer
No 8 on p. 159 – for a steadfast faith in the Trinity.

Extras

Bible study
Galatians 5:16–26.

In a group
Everyone should list the names of the other group members; then beside each name privately write down one quality from the list of the 'fruit of the Spirit' (Galatians 5:22, 23) which you can clearly see in that person. When all are ready, each take it in turn to listen to the others say what quality they can see the Holy Spirit developing in you. Respond with a simple 'Thank you'. When all are finished, silently thank God that he is refining our characters in ways that others can see even when we are not aware of it ourselves.

Response
Express your praise to God for his Holy Spirit in any way that is meaningful for you. This might be writing a prayer or poem; drawing a picture; singing or composing a song...

Check-up
Do you ask God to fill you with his Spirit each day?

Suggestions for further reading
Billy Graham, *The Holy Spirit* (Collins, 1978). A thorough and readable introduction to the person and ministry of the Holy Spirit.
J.I. Packer, *Keep in Step with the Spirit* (IVP, 1984). A scholarly evaluation of 'charismatic' and other claims in the light of Scripture.

Christian Behaviour

Your confirmation is a brief service, which is all over in an hour or so; its implications should last a lifetime. Your confirmation takes place in a religious building; it works itself out in the secular world – in home and college, job and community. Your confirmation entails giving required answers to set questions; its real concern is not with what you say in church but with how you live subsequently.

7. Moral Standards

As we turn from Christian belief to Christian behaviour, and in this chapter to the standards which Christ expects from his followers, we are immediately aware of a conflict between his way and the way of the world. In our era in the West good and evil are being redefined and relativized. Whether we are thinking of business ethics, of respect for the sanctity of human life, of sex, home and family, or of the greed of consumerism, the boundaries of what is acceptable are being steadily extended. The fact is that once the Christian faith has been abandoned, the Christian ethic will not long survive.

God's call to his people in every age is to be radically different from the prevailing culture in their values, standards and lifestyle. 'You must not do as they do in Egypt, where you used to live', God told Moses to say to Israel, 'you must not do as they do in the land of Canaan where I am bringing you. Do not follow their practices. You must obey my laws and be careful to follow my decrees. I am the Lord your God' (Leviticus 18:1–4). The New Testament equivalent to this instruction seems to be Jesus' word to his followers in the Sermon on the Mount. They were surrounded by both religious people (Pharisees) and irreligious people (pagans). But they were to copy neither. 'Do not be like them', Jesus said (Matthew 6:8). Instead, they were to follow his teaching and his example.

The Ten Commandments

The summary statement of his standards, which God revealed to his people, was the Ten Commandments. They are still in force.

The traditional site of the Sermon on the Mount.

Even though the Old Testament ceremonial law is now obsolete (its sacrifices, dietary regulations, etc.), and its civil law (both statutes and sanctions) is not necessarily appropriate for nations today, yet its moral law stands. It is not just the law of Moses, but the law of God. What Jesus did in the Sermon on the Mount was not to repeal the moral law, but to interpret it. In the six antitheses ('you have heard that it was said ... , but I tell you ...') (Matthew 5:21–48), what Jesus was contradicting was not the law of Moses but the scribal distortions of it, which attempted to make it easier to obey. Instead, Jesus drew out the radical implications of God's law.

'But', somebody protests, 'surely Paul wrote that we are "not under law"? Did he not mean that the law has been abolished for Christians?' The answer to the first question is 'yes', and to the second 'no'. It is very important to understand Paul correctly. He meant (1) that we are 'not under law' for our justification, but rather 'under grace', (Romans 6:14,15), in the sense that God accepts us because of his mercy and not our merit, and (2) that we are 'not under law' for our sanctification, but rather 'led by the Spirit' (Galatians 5:18), in the sense that God makes us holy by the power of his Spirit within us, and not by our own unaided efforts. But we are still 'under Christ's law' (1 Corinthians 9:21) in the sense that we are under obligation to obey it. Indeed, God sent his Son to die for us 'in order that the righteous requirements of the law might be fully met in us' (Romans 8:3, 4), and God puts his Spirit within us in order to write his law in our hearts (2 Corinthians 3:3). This explains an extraordinary fact about God's Old Testament promise of the Messianic age. He expressed it by saying both 'I will put my Spirit in you' (Ezekiel 36:27) and 'I will put my law in their minds and write it on their hearts' (Jeremiah 31:33).

This close connection between God's Spirit and God's law is immensely important. As we reflect on his law in this chapter, his standards will seem daunting, and even unattainable, until we remember that he also offers us his Spirit. In fact, the indwelling Spirit can enable us (1) to *know* God's law, so that we grow in our understanding of its implications for today, (2) to *love* God's law, so that we see it no longer as a burden but as a delight ('Oh, how I love your law!' – Psalm 119:97), and (3) to *do* God's law, so that, freed from slavery to sin, we find in obedience the true freedom. God does not make demands without also making provision for us to meet them.

Jesus summed up the moral law in terms of love. He brought together the commands to love God with all our being (Deuteronomy 6:5) and to love our neighbour as ourselves (Leviticus 19:18), which nobody had done before, and added 'there is no commandment greater than these', for 'all the law and the prophets hang on these two commandments' (Matthew 22:37–40; cf. Mark 12:31). We have to learn therefore to understand and apply God's commandments in the light of the requirements of love, noting in particular that the single, positive and comprehensive principle of love embraces and even transcends the many negative and specific precepts of the law. Moreover, the love Jesus had in mind was neither sentimental nor selfish, but strong and sacrificial. What we call love is usually *erōs*, the desire to obtain and possess, whereas God's love is *agapē*, the desire to give and to enrich. To love is to sacrifice oneself in the service of others, and where there is neither sacrifice nor service there is no love. To love God is to become absorbed in his will and glory; to love others is to become engrossed in their welfare.

View from Mount Moses, in the Sinai Desert.

Love for God

The first five commandments set out our duty to God (see Exodus 20:1–12; Deuteronomy 5:1–16).

1. *I am the Lord your God, who brought you out of Egypt, out of the land of slavery. You shall have no other gods before (or besides) me.* The introduction to the Ten Commandments is God's statement: 'I am the Lord your God, who brought you out of Egypt, out of the land of slavery' (Exodus 20:2). The first commandment follows naturally. It is because God redeemed Israel, rescuing them from their bondage and claiming them as his own by the covenant he made with them at Sinai (Exodus 19:3–6), that they are forbidden to worship other gods and required to worship him alone. God's demand for our exclusive worship is due not only to the fact that he is *our* God by redemption and covenant, however, but to the fact that he is the *only* God. 'I am the Lord, there is no other', he kept repeating later through Isaiah (Isaiah 45:6,18, 22), and 'I will not give my glory to another' (Isaiah 42:8). Some say that Israel did not reach this monotheistic faith until Isaiah taught it in the eighth century BC. But surely it is already implicit in the first commandment. To forbid Israel to have any other gods 'before' or 'besides' Yahweh (as the Hebrew word 'Jehovah' is now usually spelled) is tantamount to saying that there are no other gods, for if there were, they should be worshipped. The ground for giving Yahweh our exclusive worship is that he alone is God.

And the worship he demands is not just that we say prayers and sing hymns in church. These things are not pleasing to God in and of themselves, but only if what we express in words for an hour in church is a distillation of the continuous and comprehensive homage of our hearts. We are called to put God first always and in everything. In the Book of Revelation we are given a glimpse of heaven. Central to the vision is God's throne, the symbol of his sovereign rule, and everything else is related to it (Revelation 4–7). We are called to anticipate on earth the God-centred life of heaven. This is the meaning of 'godliness'.

2. *You shall not make for yourself an idol in the form of anything in heaven above or on the earth beneath or in the waters below. You shall not bow down to them or worship them; for I, the LORD your God, am a jealous God, punishing the children for the sin of the fathers to the third and fourth generation of those who hate me, but showing love to a thousand [generations] of those who love me and keep my commandments.*

If the first commandment requires that our worship of God be exclusive, the second requires that it shall be both true and spiritual, which idolatry never is. Jesus may well have been alluding to this when he said: 'A time is coming and has now come when the true worshippers will worship the Father in spirit and truth, for they are the kind of worshippers the Father seeks. God is spirit, and his worshippers must worship in spirit and in truth' (John 4:23, 24). First, instead of worshipping God 'in truth' (praising him for who he has revealed himself to be), idolaters have a false idea of him, for they make the foolish attempt to represent the Creator in the form of one of his own creatures (cf. Acts 17:24–31; Romans 1:21–25). Idolatrous images are mental before they are metal, and every untrue, unworthy concept of God is an idol.

Secondly, instead of worshipping God 'in spirit' (recognizing that he is spirit himself and asks for spiritual worship), idolaters become preoccupied with external, visible and tangible objects. Even the worship of the people of Israel had a constant tendency to degenerate into formalism and even blatant hypocrisy. The seventh and

The traditional site of Jesus' burial, Jerusalem.

eighth century prophets were scathing in their denunciation of Israel's empty religion, and Jesus applied their criticism to the Pharisees of his own day: 'Isaiah was right when he prophesied about you hypocrites; as it is written: "These people honour me with their lips, but their hearts are far from me"' (Isaiah 29:13; Mark 7:6). So whatever outward forms we may use in Christian worship (liturgies, processions, drama, ritual, kneeling or raising our arms), we need to ensure that they escape the charge of idolatry by passing the double test of being 'in spirit and in truth'.

In the second commandment God goes on to describe himself as 'a jealous God'. There is no need to be disturbed by this. Jealousy is a resentment of rivals, and whether it is good or evil depends on whether the rival has any right to be there. Since God is unique, and there is no other, he has the right to ask that we worship him alone.

A comment is also needed on the portrayal of God as 'punishing the children for the sin of the fathers' for several generations. It is made clear later in the Bible that God holds each of us responsible for our own sins (e.g. Ezekiel 18:1–4). Nevertheless, there is abiding and solemn truth in what the commandment says. Because of the social nature of evil, God's judgment of it cannot be confined to those who commit it. Children often suffer the consequences of their parents' sins. These may be transmitted physically (by inherited disease), socially (in the poverty caused by drunkenness or gambling), psychologically (by the tensions and conflicts of an unhappy home) and morally (in habits learned from a bad example).

3. *You shall not misuse the name of the Lord your God, for the Lord will not hold anyone guiltless who misuses his name.*
There are several ways in which it is possible to 'misuse' God's name and so break this commandment.

The first and obvious one relates to the use of bad language. The 'name' of God can refer to the words by which he has made himself known ('Lord', 'God', 'Almighty', 'Christ', 'Jesus' etc.), and to 'take his name in vain', as the King James Version translates it, includes using any of them as an expletive. To do this may not be blasphemy, in the sense of expressing deliberate contempt for God, but only a thoughtless bravado. Nevertheless, to use God's name as a swear word is an evident symptom of disrespect for him, and is incompatible with a desire to worship him. All of us may think it wise from time to time to examine, and if necessary revise, our vocabulary. If we want to be really consistent, we will probably cut out even those corruptions of God's name, which are no longer recognized as such, like 'gosh' and 'gee', which are actually euphemisms for God and Jesus.

Secondly, God's name can be misused when we make promises or take oaths. To swear something 'by Almighty God' and then break our promise is to 'swear falsely'; it betrays a serious lack of regard for God's name. Because of this some of Jesus' contemporaries became preoccupied with the right formulae to use when taking oaths. They seem to have argued that, although one must keep oaths taken in God's name, it did not matter so much if they swore 'by heaven' or 'by the earth' or by something else. Jesus rejected this distinction, pointing out that heaven is God's throne and earth his footstool, so that even these expressions contained an implicit reference to God. More than that, he urged his followers not to swear at all. Oaths are not necessary for honest people who are known to keep their promises. A simple 'yes' or 'no' is enough (Matthew 5:33–37).

Thirdly, God's name is more than a word; it is he himself as he has been revealed. We misuse his name, therefore, when our behaviour is incompatible with who he is. If we love God, we shall want to 'honour' his name by living in a way which is consistent with it; we misuse it when we contradict it.

4. Remember the Sabbath day by keeping it holy. Six days you shall labour and do all your work, but the seventh day is a Sabbath to the your God. On it you shall not do any work, neither you, nor your son or daughter, nor your manservant or maidservant, nor your animals, nor the alien within your gates. For in six days the LORD made the heavens and the earth, the sea, and all that is in them, but he rested on the seventh day. Therefore the LORD blessed the Sabbath day and made it holy.

The pattern of six days' work and one day's rest goes right back to the beginning of creation (Genesis 2:2, 3). Hence the command to 'remember' the sabbath day. God made us human beings in such a way that we need to observe this rhythm. Attempts to change it by lengthening the working week to nine or ten days (e.g. by the French revolutionaries in the eighteenth century and the Russian revolutionaries in the twentieth) did not work; in each case the state reverted to God's law. Christians cannot of course force people to go to church, and would not wish to use legislation for this purpose. But we are anxious that the law will protect people from being obliged to work on Sundays (e.g. by an indiscriminate permission for spectator sports and open shops).

God intended the sabbath for worship as well as rest. It was to be 'holy to the Lord' or (in Christian terms) 'the Lord's Day'.

Christians will want to take the fullest possible advantage of this divine provision. Our Sundays are a greatly under-appreciated means of grace. We should use their hours wisely and profitably – for church-going and fellowship with other Christians, for an extra period of Bible study, for some Christian reading, for spending time with our family, for visiting an elderly or handicapped relative, and/ or for some form of Christian service (Sunday School teaching for example, or the neglected blessing of letter writing).

The Scribes and Pharisees spoiled God's good law by encrusting it with minute regulations, in order to specify in detail what was per-mitted and what was prohibited on the sabbath. Jesus deliberately broke some of these rules, because they belonged to human tradi-tion, not Scripture. For example, he encouraged his disciples when they were hungry to pick and eat some ears of corn, which the scribes said was equivalent to reaping and was therefore forbidden on the sabbath. This led Jesus to lay down the fundamental princi-ple that 'the sabbath was made for man, not man for the sabbath' (Mark 2:23–28). So he was not a 'sabbatarian', enforcing an absolute prohibition of all activity on the sabbath. He certainly

An Arab woman cuts grain in the traditional way.

accepted the biblical principle of one day's rest and worship each week, and so should we. But he made it clear that certain kinds of work could and should be done on the sabbath, without breaching this principle – for example, works of religion (the priests in the temple – Matthew 12:5), works of mercy (healing the sick – Matthew 12:9, 10) and works of necessity (lifting a sheep out of a pit into which it has fallen – Matthew 12:11). It is legitimate to apply this teaching to the work of clergy, doctors and farmers today.

Which day of the week should we observe, then, as the day of rest and worship? The sabbath was the seventh day, and Seventh Day Adventists still insist on it today. They are fine people (I have met many of them in different countries), but I myself believe that the importance of the fourth commandment lies in the 1 – 6 rhythm, not in the identity of the day. The change to the first day of the week was to commemorate the resurrection of Jesus (John 20:19, 26), and there is evidence that this continued as the day of worship (e.g. Acts 20:7; 1 Corinthians 16:1,2).

5. *Honour your father and your mother, so that you may live long in the land the LORD your God is giving you.*

Some commentators suggest that, whereas the first four commandments relate to our duty to God, and concern his being, worship, name and day, the fifth commandment introduces our duty to our neighbour, as it concerns honouring our parents. It seems to me more appropriate, however, to regard it as belonging to our duty to God. This is partly because five commandments are then attributed to each duty, but mostly because our parents, at least while we are minors, stand in the place of God and mediate his authority to us. Certainly Paul understands the honouring of our parents to require 'obedience', and calls this both right and pleasing to Christ.[1] At the same time, he adds that, if children have a duty to their parents, parents also have a duty to their children. They must neither 'exasperate' nor 'embitter' them, but rather 'bring them up in the training and instruction of the Lord' (Ephesians 6:4; Colossians 3:21). The reciprocal nature of these duties places a firm check on the behaviour of parents.

The old 1662 catechism legitimately extended the scope of this commandment to include our duty to all those who are (in old-fashioned language) our 'governors, teachers, spiritual pastors and masters'. Unfashionable as this teaching is today, the Bible is clear that God loves order, not anarchy, and that he has established certain authority structures (especially the family and the state) which he expects his people to acknowledge. At the same time, when God delegates his authority to human beings and institutions, they have no liberty to use it to justify tyranny. Authority is never absolute. If, therefore, the human person or structure should abuse its God-given authority in defiance of God, our duty is not to submit, but to resist. As the apostles put it, 'we must obey God rather than men!' (Acts 5:29).

Some people are offended by Jesus' words that unless we 'hate' our parents and other relatives, we cannot be his disciples (Luke 14:26). It is a good example both of the dramatic way in which he taught and of the Hebrew habit of expressing a comparison by a contrast. We certainly must not interpret him literally. How could he tell us one moment to love our enemies and the next to hate our parents? The clue is found in the parallel passage in Matthew's gospel, where Jesus states that anyone who loves his parents more than he loves him (Jesus) is not worthy of him (Matthew 10:37).

As life expectancy rises in some parts of the world, and the average age of the population rises proportionately, there tends also to be an increasing number of old and infirm people who are neglected and even forgotten by their own children. It is a shocking phenomenon largely confined to the West. In Africa and Asia the extended family always finds room for the elderly. I think Paul should have the last word on this matter: 'If anyone does not provide for his relatives, and especially for his immediate family, he has denied the faith and is worse than an unbeliever' (1 Timothy 5:8).

Love for neighbour

Our duty to our neighbour is summed up negatively as 'to hurt nobody by word or deed' (Catechism), since 'love does no harm to its neighbour' (Romans 13:10). Positively, it is set forth in the Golden Rule: 'do to others what you would have them do to you' (Matthew 7:12). If we truly love people, therefore, we shall respect their rights, desire their good, and serve their highest welfare. The remaining commandments enumerate five offences against love.

6. *You shall not murder.*

The familiar Revised Standard Version translation of this commandment is 'thou shalt not kill'. Some people understand it as an absolute prohibition of taking life, including animal life. But this view is untenable, since the same law contained an elaborate sacrificial system which required the slaying and offering of animals. Others explain it as an absolute prohibition of the taking of human life, and on that ground are abolitionists (of capital punishment) and pacifists. This too is an inadmissible interpretation of the sixth commandment (although some Christians hold these positions on other grounds), since the same law provided for capital punishment in extreme cases and also authorized a 'holy war' against the Canaanites. Other English versions are right, therefore, to translate the commandment 'you shall not commit murder'. What it forbids is the unauthorized taking of human life. One of the worst sins, which was repeatedly condemned in the Old Testament was 'the shedding of innocent blood'. For Scripture insisted on the sanctity not so much of life in general as of human life, because it is the life of human beings made in the image of God. To murder was therefore an offence against God the Creator as well as against one of his special creatures. Jesus went further and applied the prohibition beyond our deeds to our words and even our thoughts. It is possible to commit murder, he taught, by unjustified anger and insult (Matthew 5:21, 22). This is the radical standard of the kingdom of God.

The sanctity of human life was the basis on which capital punishment was sanctioned in the Old Testament. 'Whoever sheds the blood of man, by man shall his blood be shed, for in the image of God has God made man' (Genesis 9:6). Capital punishment, according to the Bible, far from cheapening human life (by requiring the murderer's death), demonstrates its unique value (by demanding an exact equivalent to the death of the victim). This does not mean that capital punishment must be administered in every case of murder, for God himself protected the first murderer Cain from it (Genesis 4:13–15). I personally believe that the state should retain the authority to take life or 'bear the sword' (Romans 13:4), as a witness to what murderers deserve, but that in many (even most) cases, when there are any mitigating circumstances, the sentence should be commuted to life imprisonment.

The same principle of the sanctity of human life is at stake in situations which threaten the human embryo. Because the embryo is at the very least a human being in the making, its life should be generally inviolable. Most Christian opinion is 'pro-life' rather than 'pro-choice'. It regards the destruction of the embryo by abortion as a form of murder, except for a very few carefully defined exceptions, and believes that experimentation on human embryos should be banned by law.

War is another issue which involves the question of human life. Throughout the Christian centuries opinion has been divided between pacifists (who believe that Jesus' teaching and example prohibit all resistance to evil) and defenders of 'the just war' theory (who believe that war may be permissible as the lesser of two evils if several conditions are fulfilled). They justify war as a last resort only, however, and do not believe that the use of weapons of indiscriminate destruction (nuclear, chemical or bacterial) could ever be justified.

7. *You shall not commit adultery.*

Christians believe that sex is a good gift of the good Creator, in spite of our reputation to the contrary. We believe that from the beginning 'God created man in his own image, ... male and female' (Genesis 1:27), that our distinctive sexuality (masculinity and femininity) is therefore his creation, and that he instituted marriage (it is his idea, not ours) for the mutual fulfilment of the partners as well as for the procreation of children. God's own definition of marriage is that 'a man will leave his father and mother and be united to his wife, and they will become one flesh' (Genesis 2:24). In other words, marriage is a monogamous, heterosexual union, initiated by a public leaving of parents and consummated in sexual intercourse. Jesus himself endorsed the two Genesis texts which I have just quoted, and concluded: 'Therefore what God has joined together, let man not separate' (Mark 10:6–9). Then Paul added the beautiful truth that husband and wife in their love for one another are to reflect the relationships between Christ and his church (Ephesians 5:21–33).

It is when these great positives have been established that the biblical prohibitions make sense. It is precisely because God has instituted marriage as his own intended context for sexual enjoyment that he forbids it in all other contexts. Only adultery is explicitly condemned because, being a sexual relationship between a married person and someone other than his or her spouse, it is the most direct assault on marriage, denying the spouse the fidelity originally promised (probably by deceit as well) and damaging the children's development. But other forms of sexual immorality are implicitly included because they too undermine marriage. Fornication, which is sex between unmarried people, and must be said to include living together before marriage, is an attempt to experience love without commitment. It can also become cruel by arousing in one partner desires for a long-term relationship which the other is not prepared to fulfil. Then a homosexual partnership must be regarded by Christians (and should be by everybody) not as a legitimate alternative to a heterosexual marriage, as the 'gay' community claim, but as incompatible with God's created and natural order. The only 'one flesh' experience God has authorized is within heterosexual monogamy.

It is in order to defend the positive blessings of God's purpose in marriage that Christians are negative towards any other relationship which attempts to compete with or contradict it.

One other point: Christians refuse to accept that our sexual urges are too powerful to be controlled. To concede this would be to demean human beings to the level of animals. It is part of our Christian witness to insist that whenever we are tempted, however fiercely, God always provides 'a way out' so that we 'can stand up under it' (1 Corinthians 10:13), that sexual self-control is possible, that we must 'flee from sexual immorality', that our body is the temple of the Holy Spirit who is in us, that we are no longer our own, because we have been bought with a price, and that we must therefore honour God with our body (1 Corinthians 6:18–20).

8. *You shall not steal.*

The prohibition of theft presupposes the right to hold private property and to have it protected. An ordered and secure society depends on the recognition of a clear distinction between what is ours and what is yours. To blur that difference is always anti-social. This does not of course mean that we have absolute rights over our possessions, since on the one hand we hold them in stewardship from God and on the other we are invited to share them with the needy.

But it does mean that we must recognize other people's property rights and not interfere with them.

The commandment has a wider application than to the straightforward stealing of somebody else's goods. It covers all kinds of dishonesty, cheating, intrigue, overcharging, shady transactions, working short hours, tax evasion and dodging the customs. Christians should be known for their honesty in deed and word, so that they can be completely trusted.

If we become guilty of stealing, we have of course to pay back what we have taken. In the Old Testament restitution was more than repayment, however. For instance, 'if a man steals an ox or a sheep ..., he must pay back five head of cattle for the ox and four sheep for the sheep' (Exodus 22:1; cf. Numbers 5:7). Zacchaeus, the fraudulent tax collector, probably had this kind of legislation in mind at the time of his conversion. He said to Jesus publicly: 'Look, Lord! Here and now I give half of my possessions to the poor, and if I have cheated anybody out of anything, I will pay back four times the amount' (Luke 19:8).

To forbid stealing is also to encourage people to earn their own living, so that they will be in a position to support themselves and their family, and indeed the poor as well. Paul gives this remarkable instruction to a convert who was previously dishonest: 'he who has been stealing must steal no longer, but must work, doing something useful with his own hands, that he may have something to share with those in need' (Ephesians 4:28). From a thief to a worker to a benefactor: only the gospel could effect such a transformation!

9. *You shall not give false testimony against your neighbour.*
Commandments 6, 7 and 8 are designed to protect people's life (against the murderer), home and family (against the adulterer) and property (against the thief), while the ninth commandment protects their reputation (against the false witness). A good name is a most treasured possession; indeed, it is 'more desirable than great riches, ... better than silver or gold' (Proverbs 22:1). To take it away from somebody is a kind of robbery; to destroy it is a kind of murder.

The first context to which this commandment belongs is the law court. As the judge and jury listen to the case for the prosecution and the defence, the accused person's fate is largely in the hands of the witnesses who are called to testify on oath, and who then submit to

The business centre, downtown New York City.

questioning and cross-questioning. Perjury is an extremely heinous offence. Yet it is not unknown. Jesus is not the only prisoner who has suffered at the hands of false witnesses. False witness can also be borne in the context of the home, the work-place or the wider community, in the form of slander or malicious gossip.

The prohibition of false witness carries with it the complementary responsibility to be a true witness. Truth matters to all the followers of Jesus Christ, for he claimed to be himself the truth and said he had come to bear witness to the truth. Lies and subterfuge should be abhorrent to us. Our word should be known to be trustworthy, and above all we should bear an unashamed witness to Jesus Christ.

Both false and true witnesses are dependent on their tongue. Consequently, this commandment reminds us of the immense power of the human tongue for good or evil. It is 'a small part of the body, but it makes great boasts' and has enormous influence (James 3:1–6). So unruly is it that, although human beings have succeeded in taming 'all kinds of animals, birds, reptiles and creatures of the sea', yet 'no man can tame the tongue. It is a restless evil, full of deadly poison' (James 3:7,8). At the same time, the apostle James who writes this has also stated earlier that 'anyone who considers himself religious and yet does not keep a tight rein on his tongue, ... deceives himself and his religion is worthless' (James 1:26). So tongue-control is possible! We shall be wise to keep praying the psalmist's prayer: 'Set a guard over my mouth, O Lord; keep watch over the door of my lips' (Psalm 141:3).

10. *You shall not covet your neighbour's house. You shall not covet your neighbour's wife, or his manservant or maidservant, his ox or donkey, or anything that belongs to your neighbour.*
The last commandment is particularly important because it transforms the decalogue from a civil code into a moral law, from a preoccupation with outward behaviour to a concern for inner holiness. We cannot be prosecuted in court for covetousness, since covetousness is not an act but an attitude of the heart. Covetousness is to theft what anger is to murder and lust to adultery. It is the disposition which may later erupt into sinful, even criminal, action. Paul acknowledged the influence which this commandment had on him before his conversion. He would never have known what sin was, he wrote, but for the command 'Do not covet'. He had believed himself blameless, and was so in terms of external righteousness, but this commandment condemned him because it revealed to him the state of his heart (Romans 7:7–12).

'Covetousness is idolatry', Paul wrote in another letter (Ephesians 5:5). This makes it a sin against God as well as against human beings. It is to desire something (or someone) so much more than we desire God that we allow it to usurp his rightful place. But covetousness is also selfishness. Indeed, this commandment speaks directly to the greed of the consumer society and its cynical unconcern for the world's poor and hungry people.

The opposite to covetousness is contentment. It receives more emphasis in the New Testament than it does in the western world today. 'Keep your lives free from the love of money', we read in the Letter to the Hebrews, 'and be content with what you have, because God has said "Never will I leave you, never will I forsake you"' (Hebrews 13:5). So too Paul, in spite of his many sufferings and privations, could write: 'I have learned the secret of being content in any and every situation .... I can do everything through him who gives me strength' (Philippians 4:12, 13). Moreover, there is something fundamentally appropriate about contentment when we

Shopping centres epitomize our consumer society.

remember that we are pilgrims, travelling home to God. 'Godliness with contentment is great gain. For we brought nothing into the world, and we can take nothing out of it. But if we have food and clothing, we will be content with that' (1 Timothy 6:6–8). Here, then, is the antidote to that turbulent and destructive passion called covetousness, which the tenth commandment prohibits. It is a combination of simplicity, generosity and contentment.

The life of obedience

The Ten Commandments set us very high standards. They call us to give God our exclusive, spiritual, consistent, regular and obedient worship, and to concern ourselves with the integrity of our neighbour's life, home, property and good name. And when we grasp the radical implications of these demands, as revealed by Jesus in the Sermon on the Mount, and see them as a summons to love God with all our being and to love our neighbour as we love ourselves, we should despair. Indeed, this was God's first purpose in giving us the law, namely to expose and condemn our sins, and so rob us of all hope of self-salvation. For in this way the law may be said to drive us to Christ as the one and only, the indispensable, Saviour. But once the law has sent us to Christ to be justified, Christ sends us back to the law to be sanctified, providing we remember that it is the Holy Spirit alone who can write the law in our hearts and enable us to obey it.

We need to value increasingly the priceless gift of the indwelling Spirit. Then we will come daily to Christ, reopening our personality to him, in order that the Holy Spirit may fill and change us. We will also remember that God has himself established certain channels through which his sanctifying grace reaches us. These 'means of grace' include Bible reading, prayer, worship, fellowship and the Holy Communion service. We need to make what the Puritans called 'a diligent use of the means of grace'. For, as Bishop J. C. Ryle used to put it, there are 'no gains without pains'.

Our physical health provides a good illustration. The best way to keep well and fight infection is not to resort to patent medicines when there is an epidemic and we are exposed to germs (although that may be necessary), but rather to build up our resistance during the rest of the year by disciplined habits of diet, sleep and exercise. Just so, the real secret of fighting evil and developing holiness is not what we do in the moment of temptation (although indeed we must cry to Jesus Christ for deliverance), but rather what we do the rest of the time, building up our spiritual strength by a disciplined life in the Spirit.

To the means of grace we now turn.

---

[1] Ephesians 6:1; Colossians 3:20. Disobedience to parents is seen in the New Testament as a symptom of social disintegration (Romans 1:30; 2 Timothy 3:2).

Study guide to chapter 7

See general hints on p. 7

Basic

Questions

1. How would you answer someone who says, 'The Ten Commandments are out of date'?
2. How would you answer a Christian who says, 'I've tried living by God's standards, but I can't keep it up'?
3. Which of the Ten Commandments do you find hardest to keep or most challenging? How might the Christian friends who are closest to you help you to rise to the challenge?

Promise

Strength in temptation –
1 Corinthians 10:13.

Prayer

No 3 on p. 157 – for those newly confirmed.

Extras

Bible study

Mark 12:28–34

In a group

Divide in half. Each half dramatize for the other a scene in which a Christian has difficulties in living up to one of the Commandments. Discuss the issues it raises.

Response

Work out a simple summary of the Ten Commandments to help you remember them.

Check-up

Do you accept the Ten Commandments as God's moral standards, and try to live them out with his help?

Suggestions for further reading
C.S. Lewis, *Mere Christianity* (Collins, 1950). A standard apologetic, which includes straightforward teaching on Christian behaviour.
John R.W. Stott, *Issues Facing Christians Today* (Marshall Pickering, revised edition, 1990). Challenges the reader to develop a Christian mind on a wide range of social issues.

8. Bible Reading and Prayer

If we hope to make steady progress in our Christian life, probably nothing is more important than the discipline of having daily 'quiet times' with God. They are one of the major means of grace to which I referred at the end of the last chapter. Ideally, it is first thing in the morning and last thing at night that we should keep a sacred engagement with God, although all of us have to decide what are the best times for us. If we persevere, we will soon form a habit which nothing but illness can break.

It is specially important for young people to develop this practice. After all, about a million young Americans engage in 'transcendental meditation' daily, repeating their 'mantra' over and over again. Why should young disciples of Jesus Christ not develop the much more profitable exercise of Christian meditation? 'The loyalty of Christian youth', said William Temple in 1943, 'must be first and foremost to Christ himself. Nothing can take the place of the daily time of intimate companionship with the Lord. Make time for it somehow and secure that it is real'.

It would be a great mistake, however, to regard daily quiet times as necessary only for the young. I can myself testify, from an experience of more than fifty years, to the vital need to meet Christ in this way every day. I think too of Dr. Frank Gaebelein, headmaster for forty-one years of Stony Brook School, Long Island. Asked on his eightieth birthday what counsel he might wish to give to the next generation of Christian leaders, he replied: 'Maintain at all costs a daily time of Scripture reading and prayer. As I look back, I see that the most formative influence in my life and thought has been my daily contact with Scripture over sixty years'.[1]

'Maintain at all costs a daily time of Scripture reading and prayer.'

If these times of quiet waiting upon God are to be balanced, they will consist of Bible reading and prayer – and in that order. First, we listen to what God may have to say to us through his word. We ask him like the boy Samuel, 'Speak, Lord, for your servant is listening' (1 Samuel 3:9,10). And we seek to imitate Mary of Bethany, who 'sat at the Lord's feet listening to what he said' (Luke 10:39). Then, secondly, we speak back to him. There will be much to talk about, especially after he has spoken to us. It is like the swing of a pendulum. It is a two-way conversation, by which our relationship (even friendship) with God matures.

Bible reading

Two questions confront us as we think about the Bible. The first concerns why we should believe it to be God's word or message to us, and the second is how we should read it.

Jesus was tempted in the Wilderness of Judaea.

1. Why we should believe the Bible

The concept of 'revelation' is a fundamentally reasonable one. The word means 'unveiling' and expresses the fact that God's nature, character and purposes are hidden from us unless and until he draws the veil aside and shows himself to us. For how could our little finite minds ever penetrate into the infinite mind of God? It is impossible. He is altogether beyond us, out of reach. Here is how God himself has described the situation between us: 'For my thoughts are not your thoughts, neither are your ways my ways .... As the heavens are higher than the earth, so are my ways higher than your ways and my thoughts than your thoughts' (Isaiah 55:8, 9). If, then, God's thoughts and ways are as much higher than ours as the heavens are higher than the earth, we could never know his mind unless he should take the initiative to disclose it.

This is exactly what we believe he has done. To begin with, he has revealed himself in the created universe, as we have seen. But that is a revelation only of his glory. His grace, his undeserved love for sinners, he has not disclosed in creation, but supremely in Christ, and in the total biblical witness to Christ. Jesus Christ is God's living word, while Scripture is his written word which points us to Christ. Both are God's 'word' which he has spoken. Just as human beings can know each other's minds only if they speak to each other, so we can know God's mind only because he has spoken (cf. Hebrews 1:1, 2).

In the Old Testament, over a long period of time, and progressively, God made himself known to his covenant people, especially through his messengers, the prophets, who regularly introduced their oracles with formulae like 'The word of the Lord came to me, saying' or 'Thus says the Lord' or 'Listen to the word of the Lord'. Jesus himself took these prophetic claims at their face value. He accepted the Old Testament Scriptures as the word of his Father. The evidence for this is compelling. First, he obeyed them in his own life and countered each temptation of the devil with an apt biblical quotation. Next, he believed that the Scriptures testified to him and were fulfilled in him, and he interpreted his mission in the light of their teaching. Thirdly, he quoted them, in debate with religious leaders, as the ultimate authority, the final court of appeal. It would be very anomalous for us to have a lower view of the Old Testament than he had, for 'the disciple is not above his teacher'. The New

Testament authors had the same respect for the Old Testament as Jesus had. For example, 'all Scripture is God-breathed' (2 Timothy 3:16). This clarifies that the meaning of 'inspiration' is not that God breathed into the authors, but that he breathed their words out of his mouth. It is a dramatic metaphor for the double authorship of Scripture, namely that his words were simultaneously theirs, as theirs were simultaneously his.

Jesus not only believed the Old Testament, but made provision for the writing of the New. He chose, called, equipped, sent and inspired the apostles, giving them a ministry parallel to that of the prophets in the Old Testament. His promises to the apostles in the upper room are particularly important. On the one hand, the Holy Spirit would 'remind' them of what Jesus had taught them (John 14:16), and on the other he would 'guide' them into all the truth which he had wanted to teach them, but which they had been unable to receive (John 16:12,13). These complementary promises of the reminding and the teaching ministries of the Holy Spirit were mainly fulfilled respectively in the writing of the Gospels and the Epistles.

As for the Gospels, which tell the story of Jesus, there are several reasons why we should confidently accept their reliability. In the first place, their authors were honest Christian men, to whom truth was important, and who give evidence in their writing of their integrity and impartiality. Next, they were either themselves eye-witnesses or dependent on eye-witnesses (see e.g. Luke 1:1–4). Further, contrary to what used to be said, the four Gospels are all first century documents. Indeed an increasing number of scholars believe that they were all published before the destruction of Jerusalem in AD 70. The short gap between the events and the written account of them was bridged by the churches' use of the words and works of Jesus in their evangelism and teaching of converts. In addition, we now have so many manuscripts, versions (i.e. translations) and quotations that the original text has been accurately established. Only a few insignificant uncertainties remain.

The Bible also wonderfully seems to be what it claims to be. Its underlying unity of theme is the more impressive because it is a library of sixty-six books written by some forty authors over about 1500 years. Its Old Testament prophecies were remarkably fulfilled. Its doctrines are profound and its ethics noble. Nearly 2000 years after Christ its popularity continues to increase. It has brought forgiveness

The earliest known fragment of the New Testament.

to the guilty, freedom to the oppressed, guidance to the perplexed, consolation to the dying and hope to the bereaved. Everyone who reads it with an open mind and a humble spirit testifies to its power to disturb and to comfort. As a Chinese Christian once said, 'every time I read that book it kicks me!' The final evidence that it is the word of God is that God speaks personally to us through it.

I am not claiming that it is all equally profitable, or that it is all easy to understand. On the contrary, all Bible readers need to learn the basic principles for interpreting it. First, we look for the *natural* meaning of the text, remembering that the plain and obvious meaning is sometimes not literal but figurative. Secondly, we look for the *original* meaning. We have to avoid reading our twentieth century thoughts back into the mind of the authors. The key questions are what they themselves intended to say and how they will have been understood by their contemporaries. For this we will need to know something about the historical, geographical and cultural background of the Bible. Thirdly, we look for the *general* meaning. That is to say, we must interpret each text in the light both of its immediate context in the chapter or book concerned and of its wider context in the Bible as a whole. The twentieth of the Anglican Church's Thirty-Nine Articles is wise to forbid the church to 'so expound one place of Scripture that it be repugnant to another'. Instead, we will be right to seek harmony by allowing Scripture to interpret Scripture.

How we should read the Bible

A method of some kind is essential. It is not enough to keep reading our favourite passages. Nor should we imitate the butterfly and flit irresponsibly from verse to verse. Some Christians like to work out their own system, alternating between books of the Old and New Testaments. Others like to take time to study one particular book at some depth and find that the 'Bible Speaks Today' series (published by Inter-Varsity Press) helps them to do this. These books try both to grapple with the meaning of the biblical text and to relate it to the contemporary world. Personally, I would like to recommend the Scripture Union method.[2] They publish daily explanatory notes in many languages, graded to suit the age and experience of readers, and written by scholars who believe Scripture to be God's Word. Scripture Union takes readers through the whole Bible in five years.

Now here are four suggestions on how to read:

(1) *Pray*! Since the Bible is God's Word, we cannot read it with the casual indifference which we might give to the daily newspaper. Instead we shall approach it with 'that reverence and humility without which no-one can understand' God's truth (John Calvin). We shall also cry to the Holy Spirit to illumine our minds, and in particular to show Christ to us. The risen Lord, walking along the road to Emmaus with two of his disciples, 'explained to them what was said in all the Scriptures concerning himself' (Luke 24:27). This is how Christopher Chavasse, a former Bishop of Rochester, put it:

The Bible ... is the portrait of our Lord Jesus Christ. The Gospels are the Figure itself in the portrait. The Old Testament is the background, leading up to the divine Figure, pointing towards it, and absolutely necessary for the composition as a whole. The Epistles serve as the dress and accoutrements of the Figure, explaining and describing it. And then, while by our Bible reading we study the portrait as one great whole, the miracle happens! The Figure comes to life! And, stepping from the canvas of the written word, the everlasting Christ of the Emmaus story becomes himself our Bible teacher to interpret to us in all the Scriptures the things concerning himself.

The Holy Spirit delights, in answer to our prayers, to bring Jesus Christ alive to us in our Bible reading. Then, echoing the Emmaus disciples, we too will be able to testify that our hearts were 'burning within us while he ... opened the Scriptures to us' (Luke 24:32).

(2) *Think*! We must think as well as pray. 'Reflect on what I am saying', Paul wrote to Timothy, 'for the Lord will give you insight into all this' (2 Timothy 2:7). Only God could give insight; but Timothy had to do the reflecting. It is the same with us. We have to combine our own researches with dependence on the Holy Spirit's illumination. For this a modern study Bible like the New International Version (from which I have been quoting) will be very useful, and perhaps as well a more popular version like the Good News Bible, whose New Testament section is called 'Good News for Modern Man'. A concordance is handy to help one find a text or passage. Then a reliable one-volume commentary like the *New Bible Commentary*[3] and a coloured compendium like *The Lion Handbook to the Bible*[4] will supply us with a lot of background information. But these are only aids. Our responsibility is to read, re-read and go on reading the passage, and to worry at it like a dog

with a bone. I find it helpful to keep asking myself two questions. First, what did it mean? That is, what was its original sense? Secondly, what does it say? That is, what is its contemporary application? It is now that the basic principles of interpretation, which I mentioned earlier, will come into use.

(3) *Remember*! Whenever God speaks to us, we must try to remember what he says. A bad memory was the downfall of Israel. The people kept forgetting the lessons which God had taught them. One stimulus to the memory is a pen. It is helpful to keep a notebook in which to write down either by days, or under subject headings, or under books of the Bible, the particular truths which God teaches us. Then we will be able to refer to them from time to time and refresh our memories. Another way is to learn by heart verses which have particularly struck us. We can make a note of them and keep revising them. If we commit to memory (say) one verse a week, with its reference, our knowledge of God and his word will steadily increase.

(4) *Obey!* There is not much point in reading the Bible at all if we never put it into practice. To pray, think and remember are wasted effort if we then reject what we have learned. The wise man, according to Jesus, who builds his house so firmly on rock that even the fiercest storms cannot shake it, is someone who listens to his words 'and puts them into practice' (Matthew 7:24). James too, echoing this emphasis of Jesus, appeals to his readers to 'be doers of the word, and not hearers only' (James 1:22 RSV). He humorously likens disobedient Bible readers to people who look at themselves in the mirror, see that they need to wash their face or brush their hair, and then immediately forget to do it.

Prayer

Men and women are at their noblest and best when they are on their knees before God in prayer. To pray is not only to be truly godly; it is also to be truly human. For here are human beings, made by God like God and for God, spending time in fellowship with God. So prayer is an authentic activity in itself, irrespective of any benefits it may bring us. Yet it is also one of the most effective of all means of grace. I doubt if anybody has ever become at all Christlike who has not been diligent in prayer. 'What is the reason', asked Bishop J. C. Ryle, 'that some believers are so much brighter and holier than others?' 'I believe the difference', he answered himself, 'in nineteen cases out of twenty, arises from different habits about private prayer. I believe that those who are not eminently holy pray *little* and those who are eminently holy pray *much*.' Again, 'prayer and sinning will never live together in the same heart. Prayer will consume sin, or sin will choke prayer'.[5]

Rightly understood, prayer is always a response to God's word. He speaks first (through the Bible); we reply (in prayer). This being so, it is a good rule to begin our prayer time by talking back to him (whether in praise, confession or request) on the same subject on which he has been speaking to us in our Bible reading. To do so is only polite; it is regarded as rude to change the conversation. In practice, then, it is helpful after our reading and meditation to keep our Bible open before us and go through the passage again, verse by verse, turning it into appropriate prayer. It is always a joy to do this. In addition to being right, it helps us to translate our reading into everyday life.

In all our prayers we should be as natural as possible. We need to remember that God is our Father and we are his children. A middle-aged cook in a government department once said to me: 'I find you can talk to God kind of confidential-like. You can tell 'im some of your secrets – just between you and 'im alone'. She was right. At the same time, we should not allow our familiarity with God to degenerate into irreverence. Nor should we imagine that colloquial language is necessarily best. Many Christians prefer to use set forms of prayer, and love to echo well-phrased prayers from the past. There are several good books of prayers available. Others like to make their own collection and add some of their own compositon. A selection of prayers on different topics is included at the end of this book.

There are at least five different kinds of prayer, all of which should find a place in our private devotions. One way to distinguish between them is to note that in each we are looking in a different direction.

(1) The look up at God.
This is *worship*. It is to seek to give to God the glory which is due to his name. Indeed, the best biblical definition of worship I know is to 'glory in his holy name' (Psalm 105:3), that is, to revel in the unique wonder of who he is and has revealed himself to be. If worship is right because God is worthy of it, it is also the best of all antidotes

to our own self-centredness, the most effective way to 'disinfect us of egotism', as one writer put it long ago.[6] In true worship we turn the searchlight of our mind and heart upon God and temporarily forget about our troublesome and usually intrusive selves. We marvel at the beauties and intricacies of God's creation. We 'survey the wondrous cross on which the Prince of glory died'. We are taken up with God, the Father, the Son and the Holy Spirit. Jesus taught us to do this in the Lord's Prayer, whose first three sentences focus not on our needs but on his glory, on the honouring of his name, the spread of his kingdom and the doing of his will. Because we are normally so turned in on ourselves, we will not find this easy. But we have to persevere, since nothing is more right or more important.

One help to concentration in worship is to use a hymn book, and to sing or say some of the great objective hymns like 'Holy, holy, holy, Lord God Almighty', 'Immortal, invisible, God only wise' or 'O worship the King all glorious above'. They fix our attention on God's being and character, and on his mighty works of creation and redemption. By contrast, too many modern hymns are unhealthily taken up with ourselves, our own needs and our own experiences. Not all by any means, however. I think for example of Bishop Timothy Dudley Smith's paraphrase of the Magnificat, 'Tell out, my soul, the greatness of the Lord' and Canon Michael Saward's 'King of the Universe, Lord of the ages'.

(2) **The look in at ourselves.**

This leads to *confession*. We all know that too much introspection can be unhealthy, unhelpful and even damaging. But some is not only salutary, but necessary. Our Bible reading will often sober and abase us in this way. The word of God ruthlessly exposes our sin, selfishness, vanity and greed, and then challenges us to repent and to confess. One of the safest ways to do this is to take on our lips one of the penitential psalms, especially perhaps Psalm 51 ('Have mercy on me, O God') or Psalm 130 ('Out of the depths I cry to you, O Lord').

It is a healthy discipline each evening to review the day briefly and call to mind our failures. Not to do so tends to make us slapdash about sin and encourages us to presume on God's mercy, whereas to make a habit of doing so humbles and shames us, and increases our longing for greater holiness. There is nothing morbid

In true worship we 'survey the wondrous cross on which the Prince of glory died.'

about the confession of sins, so long as we go on to give thanks for the forgiveness of sins. It is fine to look inwards, so long as it leads us immediately to look outwards and upwards again.

(3) The look round at others.

This is *intercession*. Jesus set us an example by praying both for his disciples and for his enemies. Paul prayed for his converts (for many of them by name), for the churches he had founded, and also for Christians he had never met (e.g. Romans 1:8–10; Colossians 2:1). We too should include other people in our prayers; it may be the best service we can render them.

Many Christians keep a prayer list of some kind. It helps to make us methodical. On it we will probably include our family and friends, relatives and godchildren, associates at work, and the leaders and members of our church. We shall want too to remember from time to time the royal family, our government and parliament, other national leaders who are influential in public life, and particular people who are featuring in the newspapers. Our Christian concern for peace and justice in the world, and for world evangelization, will also undoubtedly express itself in our prayers. It would be easy to make our list so long as to be burdensome and even unmanageable. One way to avoid this is to pray for a few special people daily, for others weekly, and then to keep a longer list of those we want to remember once a month or from time to time. Whatever system we adopt, it is sensible to keep it elastic and adaptable. I like to keep a special note of people who have asked me to pray for them in relation to a particular need – somebody facing an exam or an operation perhaps, somebody who is very near the kingdom of God or has just come to Christ, or somebody facing an important decision or going through a time of special stress. Then, as different crises arise and pass, it is natural to add some people to the list and cross others off it. The more specific and concrete we can be in our prayers, the better. To make a note of our prayers also increases our expectation, as we look to God for answers.

(4) The look back to the past.

This should lead to *thanksgiving*, which differs from worship. In worship we praise God for who he is in himself; in thanksgiving we acknowledge gratefully what he has done for us and for others.

Israel's forgetfulness led to ingratitude. The people had been urged to remember all God's kindness to them, 'but they soon forgot what he had done' (Psalm 106:13). Hopefully, we will not make the same mistake. It is good to talk to ourselves and to exhort ourselves to remembrance and to thanksgiving, as the psalmist did: 'Praise the Lord, O my soul, and forget not all his benefits' (Psalm 103:2).

The General Thanksgiving in the Prayer Book provides a wonderfully comprehensive summary of what to thank God for – first 'for our creation, preservation and all the blessings of this life', then 'above all for your immeasurable love in the redemption of the world by our Lord Jesus Christ', but also 'for the means of grace, and for the hope of glory' (that is, the assurance of heaven in the end). At the close of each day it seems right to look back over it in order to recall not only our sins but also God's mercies. If we confess the former, we must not forget to thank God for the latter.

(5) **The look on to the future.**

This is *petition* or *supplication*. I have left it to the last, although it looms largest in the prayers of most of us. Indeed, we should not be ashamed to bring our requests to God (Philippians 4:6). Jesus himself told us to come to our heavenly Father and acknowledge our dependence upon him for our daily food, the forgiveness of our sins and our deliverance from evil.

But God knows our needs; we do not need to tell him. And in his love he wants to supply them; we do not need to bully or badger him. So why pray? What is the point? John Calvin gave a thorough answer to these questions. He wrote:

Believers do not pray with the view of informing God about things unknown to him, or of exciting him to do his duty, or of urging him as though he were reluctant. On the contrary, they pray in order that they may arouse themselves to seek him, that they may exercise their faith in meditating on his promises, that they may relieve themselves from their anxieties by pouring them into his bosom; in a word, that they may declare that from him alone they hope and expect, both for themselves and for others, all good things.[7]

The purpose of petitionary prayer, then, is neither to inform God as though he were ignorant, nor to persuade him as though he were reluctant. It is not to bend God's will to ours, but rather to align our will to his. Our Father does not spoil his children. He waits until we desire his will.

We look, therefore, into the future. We anticipate the duties and problems, hopes and fears, of tomorrow, next week, next year. We peer further ahead to possible sickness and bereavement, to our death, to the Parousia, the Resurrection, the new heaven and the new earth. Uncertainties attend all these events, whether and when and how they will take place. What is our wish, then, our prayer? Christians have only one: 'not my will but yours be done'. We ask for guidance to know God's will and for strength to do it.

We have seen that the Christian life is a life of prayer. It is a Trinitarian experience of communion with the Father through the Son by the Spirit. And it is essentially a response to God's word. The more disciplined we become in our set times of devotion, the more easy it will be to 'pray continually' (1 Thessalonians 5:17) and to 'abide in Christ' (John 15:1–8). For a sense of his presence will permeate the periods in between.

---

[1] From an interview with him published in *Christianity Today* on 20th April 1979.

[2] The Scripture Union, 130 City Road, London EC1V 2NJ.

[3] IVP, 3rd edition, 1970.

[4] Revised edition, 1983.

[5] From a chapter entitled 'Do you pray?' in *Home Truths* by J.C. Ryle, undated, pp. 114 and 121.

[6] Quoted by W. E. Sangster in *The Pure in Heart: A Study in Christian Sanctity* (Epworth, 1954), p. 201.

[7] From Calvin's exposition of Matthew 6:8 in his *Commentary on a Harmony of the Evangelists* (1558).

Study guide to chapter 8

See general hints on p. 7

Basic

Questions

1. How would you answer someone who says, 'The Bible is out of date'?
2. How would you answer a Christian who says, 'I've tried praying, but it doesn't seem to work'?
3. How helpful do you find your present practice of reading the Bible and praying? In what ways might you be able to make it more helpful?

Promises

Answered prayer – John 15:7.
Peace of mind – Philippians 4:6, 7.

Prayers

No 9 on p. 159 – for the reading of the Bible.
No 10 on p. 159 – for help in learning to pray.

Extras

Bible study

Luke 24:13–32

In a group

Study Luke 24:13–32 together using the Pray – Think – Remember suggestions on pp. 117–118. How will you then help each other to Obey?

Response

Spend some time in prayer, using the five 'directions' outlines on p. 119–124.

Check-up

Do you read the Bible and pray regularly, ideally every day?

Suggestions for further reading

Valuable Reference Books
The Lion Handbook to the Bible (Lion, revised edition, 1983).
Donald Guthrie, *New Testament Introduction* (IVP, 1970).
The New Bible Dictionary (IVP, revised edition, 1982), or the three volume version.
The Illustrated Bible Dictionary (IVP, 1980).
Bible reading
John R. W. Stott, *Understanding the Bible* (Scripture Union, 1984). Chapters covering the history, geography, authority, message, interpretation and use of the Bible.
Prayer
John White, *People in Prayer* (IVP, 1977). An illuminating study of ten biblical characters.
O. Hallesby, *Prayer* (1948; IVP reprint). A simple but profound Christian classic.

9. Fellowship and the Holy Communion

If the first condition of Christian health and progress is that we maintain a close relationship with God through daily Bible reading and prayer, the second is that we maintain close fellowship with one another in the Christian community. The Christian life cannot be lived in isolation (except in the unlikely event of finding ourselves marooned on a desert island!). Nor, indeed, once we have tasted the joys of fellowship, shall we ever want to cut ourselves off from it.

Fellowship

Yet many people, not least new converts, find the prospect of church membership uninviting and even positively embarrassing. They feel decidedly ill at ease in the church. The ideal of a multi-cultural community sounds great; but the reality they experience falls far short of it. Nobody has expressed this feeling of awkwardness vis-à-vis the church more pungently than C. S. Lewis. When he began, after his conversion to theism, to attend his parish church on Sundays and his college chapel on weekdays, he wrote that he found the idea of being a churchman 'wholly unattractive'. He continued:

Though I liked clergymen as I liked bears, I had as little wish to be in the church as in the zoo. It was, to begin with, a kind of collective; a wearisome 'get-together' affair .... To me, religion ought to have been a matter of good men praying alone and meeting by twos and threes to talk of spiritual matters. And then the fussy, time-wasting botheration of it all! – the bells, the crowds, the umbrellas, the notices, the bustle, the perpetual arranging and organising. Hymns were (and are) extremely disagreeable to me. Of all musical instru-

ments I liked (and like) the organ least. I have, too, a sort of spiritual gaucherie which makes me unapt to participate in any rite.[1]

Those of us who have been church members for many years, even all our lives, find it difficult to appreciate the painful temperamental and cultural adjustments which new converts often have to make. Some others, of course, have no such problem. They move out of their pre-conversion alienation into a community of acceptance which they have never experienced before, and which brings them nothing but relief and exultation. It is those with difficulties I am concerned for now. We need to be more sensitive and sympathetic towards them, and do our best to make their transition into the Christian community as painless as possible. Yet we must also encourage them to persevere, since committed membership of the church is an indispensable (and, once the adjustment has been made, exceedingly joyful) part of our Christian discipleship. As John Wesley once put it, 'to turn Christianity into a solitary religion is to destroy it'. To be sure, it has a solitary aspect (a personal relationship to God through Christ), but it has a social aspect too (fellowship with other believers). The same Jesus in the same Sermon on the Mount, who encouraged us to engage in private prayer ('When you pray, go into your room, close the door and pray to your Father ... in secret' – Matthew 6:6), also told us when we pray to say 'Our Father' (Matthew 6:9), which we can do only when we are together.

Members of his body

God's purpose, which was conceived in a past eternity, is being worked out in history, and will be perfected in the eternity still to come, is not to save individual souls in isolation from one another, and so perpetuate our loneliness, but to build a church, to gather together into one a people of his own, drawn from every nation and culture. The New Testament portrays this divine society by many vivid metaphors. We are sisters and brothers in God's family, citizens of his kingdom, and stones in his temple (e.g. Ephesians 2:19–22). We are also the sheep of Christ's flock, the branches of his vine and the members of his body (e.g. John 10:14–16; 15:1–8; 1 Corinthians 12:27). We belong irrevocably to one another because we belong irrevocably to him.

This is not a statement of faith only, but of fact. I can myself testify to it from experience. Having had the privilege of much travel,

I have met fellow Christians on all six continents. I have worshipped with them in some of the great medieval cathedrals of Europe, in makeshift tin huts in Latin American villages, with Eskimos in the Canadian Arctic, and under trees in the tropical heat of Africa and Asia. I have been lovingly welcomed by sisters and brothers in Christ, always with a smile and often also with a hug or a kiss, even when we have never met before and even when our respective languages have been mutually incomprehensible. The fact is that the Christian church is the biggest family on earth, and the only multi-racial, multi-national, multi-cultural community that exists. I am told that when Margaret Mead, the well-known American anthropologist, saw in Vancouver in 1983 the thousands of Christians from all over the world who had gathered for the Sixth Assembly of the World Council of Churches, she exclaimed 'you are a sociological impossibility!'. But what is impossible to human beings is possible to God. Through Jesus Christ he has broken down the barriers which divided us, and by reconciling us to himself has reconciled us to one another.

The Christian fellowship is not only an article of faith and a glorious reality; it is also an enormous help. Our church membership exerts a stabilizing influence on us. Just as the human family provides support for its young people when they are passing through the turbulent years of adolescence, so the divine society can keep us steady when we are assailed by temptation, tribulation or doubt. Or let me change the metaphor. A Scottish minister was visiting a church member who had recently absented himself from Sunday worship. He sat in silence before the fire. After a while he lent forward, picked up the hearth tongs, took a burning coal from the fire, and laid it in the fireplace. It flickered briefly and went out. The minister then picked it up and put it back with the other coals. Within a few seconds it was on fire again. The minister took his leave, having said nothing throughout his visit. But the absentee was back in church the following Sunday.

In all probability my reader is already an active member of a local church and indeed is preparing to become a full member by confirmation. If by any chance you are not, however, I would like to urge you to remedy this as soon as possible. It is entirely anomalous, if not actually impossible, to claim membership of the universal, invisible church without belonging to a local, visible manifestation of it.

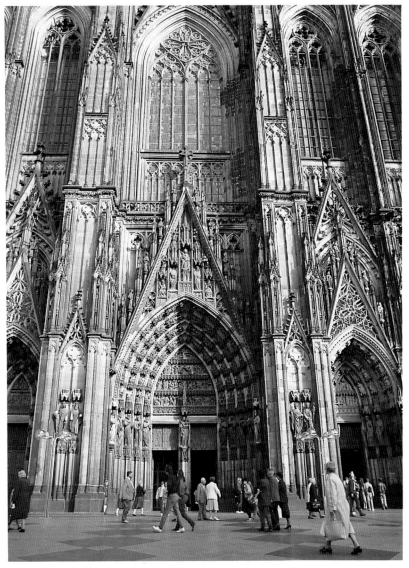

We can worship in a great cathedral – or a tin hut.

I beg you also not to be an ecclesiastical gypsy, always on the move from church to church, and having no fixed abode! Instead, I hope you will join a church, settle down in it, introduce yourself to others, and always be in your place for Sunday worship. If your circumstances permit, it is good to attend one of the church's midweek activities too, whether a central Bible study or prayer meeting or (better still) a neighbourhood fellowship group of a dozen or so people. It is in such smaller gatherings that members get to know one another and can encourage one another in the Lord.

Although like Jesus, who was nicknamed 'the friend of tax collectors and sinners', we ought to have a wide circle of friends who are not believers, we will now find that in Christ we can experience deeper friendships than we have known previously. As Bishop Stephen Neill has written, 'friendship between the friends of Jesus of Nazareth is unlike any other friendship'.[2] Those of us who have enjoyed the blessings of a close Christian friendship will want to stress the value of what older writers called a 'soul friend', with whom we can share our doubts and fears, problems and temptations, joys and hopes. Also, assuming that some of my readers are single, I need to say that Christians who decide to marry are at liberty to marry only Christians, for the 'unequal yoke' between a Christian and a non-Christian is forbidden (2 Corinthians 6:14). Marriage is too close and sacred a union to be physical, social and intellectual, but not spiritual.

The Holy Communion

The chief expression of fellowship between Christian people is the Holy Communion service. Paul called it 'the Lord's Supper' (1 Corinthians 11:20), which indicates what it is, namely the fellowship meal of disciples, by invitation of their Lord. Instituted by Jesus himself during his last evening on earth, most churches have recognized it ever since as the heart of Christian worship. Luke seems to indicate that, at least in Asia Minor in AD 57, it was the churches' custom on the first day of each week to assemble in order 'to break bread' (Acts 20:7). The Lord's Day would have been incomplete without the Lord's Supper. Many Anglican churches this century have been seeking to recover its centrality by making it the main Sunday service. Others believe they can best emphasize its importance by holding a Communion service for the whole church family on one Sunday a month.

The Old Testament equivalent of the Holy Communion service was the Passover, even though it was celebrated only once a year. The Israelites were given the instruction that 'When your children ask you "What does this ceremony mean to you?"', they were to explain its origins at the time of the exodus from Egypt (Exodus

'Do this in remembrance of me.'

12:25–27). Similarly, it is important for us to ask and answer questions about the meaning of the Holy Communion. I am going to suggest that it has four main themes. You may find my explanations too analytical for your taste, and perhaps too controversial as well. But if we are to continue attending the service regularly, and if our appreciation of it is to keep growing, we need to reflect on its meaning and to face the differences of interpretation.

1. Remembrance

The simplest and most obvious meaning of the Lord's Supper is that it commemorates the death of Jesus Christ on the cross. According to the earliest account of its institution, which Paul preserved, Jesus took and broke bread, referred to it as his body, and said 'Do this in remembrance of me'. In the same way, after supper, he took a cup, referred to it as 'the new covenant in my blood' and repeated the command 'Do this, whenever you drink it, in remembrance of me' (1 Corinthians 11:23–25). Thus both by what he did with the bread and wine (breaking the one, pouring the other) and by what he said about them ('this is my body, this is my blood'), he was drawing attention to his death and its purpose, and urging them to remember him in this way.

The Anglican church has always recognized the value of this remembrance. The third exhortation in the 1662 service reads:

To the end that we should alway remember the exceeding great love of our Master and only Saviour Jesus Christ, thus dying for us, and the innumerable benefits which by his precious blood-shedding he hath obtained to us, he hath instituted and ordained holy mysteries, as pledges of his love, and for a continual remembrance of his death, to our great and endless comfort.

More simply, the old catechism stated that the Lord's Supper was ordained 'for the continual remembrance of the sacrifice of the death of Christ, and of the benefits which we receive thereby'. In order to stimulate our minds and memories, the officiating minister both copies the actions and repeats the words of Jesus in the upper room. It is essential that what he says is audible, and what he does visible, to the congregation, so that we may look, listen, understand and remember, just as the apostles must have done at the Last Supper.

2. Participation

Jesus did more than take and break bread, and take and pour wine, saying 'this is my body, this is my blood'; he also gave the elements to the apostles, saying 'take, eat and drink'. Thus they were not only spectators of the drama (watching and listening), but participants in it (eating and drinking). Just so today the Lord's Supper is more than a 'commemoration', by which we recall an event of the past; it is a 'communion', by which we share in its present benefits. This was the apostle Paul's emphasis when he wrote: 'Is not the cup of thanksgiving for which we give thanks a participation in the blood of Christ? And is not the bread that we break a participation in the body of Christ?' (1 Corinthians 10:16).

From this it is clear beyond dispute that in some sense at Holy Communion we are meant to 'participate' in Christ's body and blood. But two questions now confront us. First, *in what* do we actually participate? Secondly, *how* do we participate in it?

First, *in what* according to God's purpose do we participate at the Lord's Supper? The answer must be 'the body and blood of Christ'. But what does this mean? It means the death of Jesus Christ, together with the benefits which he obtained for us by his death. It is important to be clear about this because some people teach that

'This is my body given for you.'

'the body and blood of Christ' mean his life, not his death. Since our body is the instrument of our personality, they argue, and since our blood is the carrier of life-giving oxygen, therefore Christ's body and blood together symbolize his living personality, and it is this that we receive at Communion. But this is not what Jesus himself said. He spoke of his body not as it lived in Palestine but as it was to be 'given' on the cross, and of his blood not as it flowed in his veins while he lived but as it was to be 'shed' in his sacrificial death. Thus 'the body and blood of Christ' is a figure of speech for the benefits of his death, not for the power of his life.

Secondly, *how* do we participate in Christ's body and blood? The Catholic answer to this question is that the 'inner reality' of the bread and wine is changed into the body and blood of Christ (traditionally called 'transubstantiation'), so that to eat and drink the elements is *ipso facto* to partake of Christ. The Anglican Articles reject this, however. Article 28 declares both that transubstantiation cannot be proved from Scripture, and that it overthrows the nature of a sacrament by confusing the sign with the thing signified. Article 29 says that those who lack a living faith, even though they receive the sacrament, 'yet in no wise are they partakers of Christ'. If, then, it is not by eating and drinking that we receive Christ, how is it? It is by faith, of which eating and drinking are a vivid picture. For just as by eating the bread and drinking the wine we take them into our bodies and assimilate them, so by faith we feed on Christ crucified in our hearts and make him our own. Thus, to return to Article 28, it states that those who 'rightly, worthily and with faith' receive the sacrament also partake of Christ's body and blood, and that 'the means whereby the body of Christ is received and eaten in the Supper is faith'. Similarly, the famous sixteenth century Anglican theologian Richard Hooker wrote: 'The real presence of Christ's most blessed body and blood is not to be sought for in the sacrament, but in the worthy receiver of the sacrament'.[3]

As we saw in an earlier chapter, the sacraments have been given to us in order to stimulate our faith. In fact, they are means of grace mainly because they are means to faith. And the Lord's Supper is a means to faith because it sets forth in dramatic visual symbolism the good news that Christ died for our sins in order that we might be forgiven. Hugh Latimer, the great preacher of the English Reformation, explained this symbolism during his trial in Oxford, before going to the stake:

There is a change in the bread and wine, and such a change as no power but the omnipotency of God can make, in that that which before was bread should now have the dignity to exhibit Christ's body. And yet the bread is still bread, and the wine is still wine. For the change is not in the nature but the dignity. [4]

This is sometimes called 'transignification', in distinction to 'transubstantiation', for the change which is in mind is one of significance, not of substance. As the officiant offers the bread and wine to our bodies, so Christ offers his body and blood to our souls. Our faith looks beyond the symbols to the reality they represent, and even as we take the bread and wine, and feed on them in our mouths by eating and drinking, so we feed on Christ crucified in our hearts by faith. The parallel is so striking, and the corresponding words of administration are so personal, that the moment of reception becomes to many communicants a direct faith-encounter with Jesus Christ. This was so, for example, in the case of John Wesley's mother, Susanna, just over a year following her son's conversion. As the cup was given to her she heard the minister saying 'the blood of our Lord Jesus Christ, which was given for thee', and at that moment 'the words struck through my heart, and I knew God for Christ's sake had forgiven me all my sins'. [5]

3. Fellowship

Five times in 1 Corinthians 11, in the space of eighteen verses, the apostle Paul uses the verb to 'come together' in relation to the Holy Communion. He seems to have regarded the Lord's Supper as the main gathering together of the Lord's people on the Lord's Day. This is still the case. And the arrangement of the furniture at Communion should facilitate it. Already the 1662 Prayer Book directed that the Holy Table 'shall stand in the body of the church or in the chancel'. It was intended that the congregation would kneel round it, like a family gathered for a meal. Unfortunately, Archbishop Laud (1633–1645) directed that Communion tables (partly because they were not always treated with proper respect) should be placed against the east wall of the chancel and railed off. In recent years, however, many churches have been re-structured in such a way that at Communion the table is brought down into the nave and the people are able to gather round the action. And as we stand or kneel right round the table, men and women, parents and children, from different racial and social backgrounds, we express and experience our undifferentiated unity in Christ.

The breaking of the bread demonstrates this. It is not just that for centuries in middle eastern culture to 'break bread together' is the way in which people pledge and cement their commitment to one another. It is also that the nature and means of our unity are symbolized in the bread we eat. 'Because there is one loaf', Paul wrote, 'we, who are many, are one body, for we all partake of the one loaf' (1 Corinthians 10:17). In order to retain this vivid symbolism, real bread should be used rather than wafers. Each communicant then receives a fragment from the same loaf, because each is a member of the same body, the body of Christ, the church. Further, since the loaf is an emblem of our crucified Saviour, it is our common participation in him (set forth visibly in our common participation in it) which makes us one.

The Lord's Supper, which is the church's fellowship meal on earth, is also a foretaste of the heavenly feast. Paul tells us that, whenever we eat the bread and drink the cup, we 'proclaim the Lord's death until he comes'(1 Corinthians 11:26). For when he comes, he will consummate his kingdom, and the symbol will give way to the reality.

4. Thanksgiving

'Eucharist' (*eucharistia* being the Greek word for thanksgiving) was from very early days a name for the Lord's Supper, and it is increasingly used in our day. Indeed, this service is an appropriate occasion on which to thank God for all his mercies, in creation and providence as well as in redemption. At the same time, as we have seen, it is Christ's death on which we should be concentrating, since this is what speaks to us from both the elements. They were not intended by Jesus to be symbols of *our* work (bread and wine being manufactured by human beings out of wheat and grapes), but of *his* (his body given and blood shed on the cross). Therefore, the focus of our thanksgiving at the Eucharist should be God's wonderful love for us in the death of his Son in our place and in the salvation which he has procured for us in consequence.

It is in this sense that the Lord's Supper is, or rather includes, a 'sacrifice'. For in the course of the service we ask God to accept 'this

'I will not drink again of the fruit of the vine until that day when I drink it anew in the kingdom of God' (Mark 14:25).

our sacrifice of praise and thanksgiving'. I confess that, having been confirmed while I was at school, I used to think of the Holy Communion as a 'sacrifice' because it took place at 8 o'clock on Sunday morning and it seemed to me a considerable sacrifice to get up so early in order to attend it!

What is meant, then, by 'eucharistic sacrifice'? In what sense may the Eucharist be regarded as a sacrifice or offering? The traditional Catholic answer is that it is an offering of Christ to God. During the third meeting of the Council of Trent (1562–3) it was affirmed that in the sacrifice of the mass 'the same Christ is contained and is bloodlessly immolated, who once offered himself bloodily on the cross, and ... that this sacrifice is propitiatory ...'.[6] This notion, that on the altar at mass Christ is offered to God as a propitiatory sacrifice for sins, was rejected by the Reformers, who were determined to go back to Scripture. They saw the Catholic mass as derogatory to the unique and wholly satisfactory sacrifice of Christ on the cross. So, in order to be consistent, they carefully excluded from the Prayer Book every use of the word 'altar' and replaced it with 'the Holy Table', 'the Lord's Table' or simply 'the Table'. For they saw the officiant at Communion not as a priest sacrificing at an altar, but as a minister serving at a table.[7] He administers a sacrament to the people; he does not offer a sacrifice to God.

In our day, although the Roman Catholic church has not officially rescinded the canons of the Council of Trent, they are trying to re-state their doctrine of eucharistic sacrifice in terms which are less offensive to the Protestant conscience. They affirm unequivocally that Christ's death 'was the one, perfect and sufficient sacrifice for the sins of the whole world' and that 'there can be no repetition of, or addition to, what was then accomplished once for all by Christ'.[8] But they also speak (as do Anglican Catholics) of the church being drawn up into Christ's self-offering, so that we share in it. This language is dangerously ambiguous, however. For we participate in Christ's sacrifice only in the sense that we share in the benefits of it, not in the sense that we share in the offering of it.

What, then, is the relation between Christ's sacrifice and us? It is multiple. We remember his sacrifice with adoring gratitude. We partake by faith of its saving benefits. We enjoy with one another the fellowship which it has made possible. And we offer ourselves to God in responsive self-sacrifice. But we do not and cannot share in Christ's offering of himself. To suggest this is to confuse what must be kept distinct, namely his offering and ours, 'the perfect and the tainted, the atoning and the eucharistic, the divine initiative and the human response'.[9]

The structure of the service

For nearly 300 years the Book of Common Prayer (1662) united the Anglican Communion, and its service of Holy Communion was the only one authorized. In 1958, however, the Lambeth Conference acknowledged that every Anglican province must be free to develop its own eucharistic liturgy. Since then, although the Book of Common Prayer has remained a foundation document, whose teaching is normative for Anglicans, many provinces have produced their own alternative prayer books. Prominent among them is the Church of England's 'Alternative Service Book' (1980). Because of this multiplicity of services and the different options which they permit, it is no longer possible to speak of a single, uniform structure. Nevertheless, a general pattern is common to all Anglican Communion services. They are divided into three parts – Antecommunion (the preparation of the congregation), Communion (the Eucharistic Prayer, followed by the distribution of the elements) and Post-communion (the final prayer and dismissal of the people).

1. Antecommunion

Cranmer took very seriously the conditions on which sinners may be encouraged to come to the Table of the Lord. Some think that he overdid the penitential preparation, and all of us welcome the mood of celebratory joy which permeates modern liturgies. It is arguable, however, that this has been an over-reaction. It is not easy to combine repentance and rejoicing in the same service. At all events, Cranmer's threefold preparation is still discernible in most services. The old catechism summed it up well, in reply to the question 'What is required of them who come to the Lord's Supper?' The answer given was: 'examine themselves, whether they *repent* them truly of their former sins, steadfastly purposing to lead a new life; have a lively *faith* in God's mercy through Christ, with a thankful remembrance of his death; and be in *charity* with all men.' Repentance, faith and love are thus delineated as the conditions of coming to the Table, and the Antecommunion gives us an opportunity to fulfil them publicly.

The regular recitation of the Ten Commandments is much to be desired in our day, since God's law is little known and much flouted. At least we need to hear Christ's summary of the law in the two commandments to love God and our neighbour. For it is the law which reveals and condemns our sin, and so calls us to repentance. Then, if the law leads us to repentance, it is the gospel which leads us to faith. So next come the reading of passages from an Epistle and a Gospel, and often nowadays an Old Testament reading as well, followed by an exposition (i.e. a sermon). After this the Nicene

Creed is said, being the response of faith to God's word read and expounded.

It is not enough to be rightly related to God in penitence and faith, however, if we are not also in right relationship with our fellow men and women. Love therefore completes the trio. It is expressed in our intercession for others, in our offerings (since it is customary for Communion gifts to be designated for the needy), and especially in the exchange of the Peace. To greet one another with 'a holy kiss' (2 Corinthians 13:12; 1 Thessalonians 5:26) or 'a kiss of love' (1 Peter 5:14) was commanded by the apostles Paul and Peter respectively. Its recent recovery in many churches (using whatever embrace or handshake is appropriate in each culture) is most welcome, so long as it can remain an authentic gesture of reconciliation in Christ.

It was only after this expression of repentance, faith and love that, in the 1662 service, the minister issued the Exhortation: 'Ye that do truly and earnestly *repent* you of your sins, and are in *love* and charity with your neighbours, ... draw near with *faith* ...'. I miss this today, or a modern equivalent, for it had the effect of 'fencing the Table' (as Presbyterians put it), of making plain the conditions for receiving Communion, although the Confession and the Prayer of Humble Access still do this to some degree. To be sure, the Table is open to sinners (otherwise who among us could approach it?), but it is *penitent* sinners who are welcome to come.

2. Communion

Immediately before the distribution of the elements comes what Cranmer called 'The Prayer of Consecration' and what most modern Anglican prayer books call 'The Eucharistic Prayer'. Cranmer's beautiful prayer, in its rolling cadences of Elizabethan English, begins with an elaborate statement of God's 'tender mercy' in the gift of his Son to die on the cross, 'who made there (by his one oblation of himself once offered) a full, perfect and sufficient sacrifice, oblation and satisfaction for the sins of the whole world'. The style could be called 'turgid' by fault-finders, but at least nobody could hear this statement Sunday by Sunday without grasping the finality and sufficiency of Christ's atoning sacrifice. Next, Cranmer introduced a prayer that those who will be receiving the bread and wine may also partake of Christ's body and blood, and concluded with the narrative of the Supper's institution, in which the officiant repeats Christ's words and actions, and so consecrates the elements to special use in Communion.

Recent Anglican liturgies have tended to follow a different pattern. They have noted the four successive actions of Jesus in the upper room. First, he 'took' the bread and wine into his hands. Secondly, he 'gave thanks'. Thirdly, he 'broke' the bread into fragments. Fourthly, he 'gave' the elements to the apostles gathered round him. This, then, is the fourfold shape which the Prayer Book revisers have given to contemporary Anglican liturgies. The president (as the officiating minister, presiding at the table, has been called at least since the middle of the second century) is first instructed to take the bread and the cup into his hands. Next, he gives thanks by leading the congregation in the Eucharistic Prayer. This ranges helpfully over the creation, the incarnation, the crucifixion, the resurrection, the exaltation and the gift of the Spirit, although in my view Christ's own emphasis on the centrality of the cross is not sufficiently accentuated. Thirdly, the president breaks the bread, which is regarded as having been consecrated by the Thanksgiving prayer, and exchanges words with the congregation which echo 1 Corinthians 10:16 and 17. Fourthly, he shares the elements with the people, usually involving others in the distribution.

3. Post-communion

Cranmer had quite an elaborate conclusion to his service, consisting of the Lord's Prayer, one or other of two Prayers of Oblation, the Gloria and the Blessing. Nearly everybody agrees that this is too long, and some would go so far as to call it an anti-climax. Its great value, however, is that the first Prayer of Oblation, which asks God 'to accept this our sacrifice of praise and thanksgiving', is deliberately separated from the Prayer of Consecration and indeed comes after the reception of the elements. In this way it is made clear beyond any doubt that our sacrifice is a grateful response to Christ's and not in any sense part of it.

Modern liturgies, in contrast to Cranmer, tend to regard the communion itself as the climax of the service, and therefore abbreviate the conclusion. In the Alternative Service Book it consists of a single prayer and a blessing. The prayer combines a thanksgiving for Christ's body and blood, an offering of ourselves to be a living sacrifice (a welcome clause) and a prayer to be sent out into the world to live to his glory. The Blessing follows, together with the dismissal 'Go in peace to love and serve the Lord'.

Our last chapter will concentrate on this service of Christ in the world.

---

[1] C. S. Lewis, *Surprised by Joy* (Geoffrey Bles, 1955; Collins reprint, 1986), pp.220–1.

[2] Stephen C. Neill, *Christian Faith Today* (Penguin, 1955), p.174.

[3] Richard Hooker, *Laws of Ecclesiastical Polity* V.67:6.

[4] Latimer, *Works* ii.286.

[5] Quoted from *The Journal of John Wesley* for 3rd September 1739.

[6] Session XXII, ch. ii.

[7] It is true that in some contexts today the word 'altar' has lost its original meaning as a place of sacrifice, as when an evangelistic appeal is termed an 'altar call' or when a man refers to his marriage to his wife as 'leading her to the altar'. Nevertheless, words and their meanings matter. In the context of Holy Communion it is surely wise for us to use 'table' in place of 'altar', in order to show that we believe the service to be a supper, not a sacrifice.

[8] The statement on *The Eucharist*, para. 5, produced by the Anglican Roman Catholic International Commission.

[9] *An Evangelical Open Letter* on ARCIC, addressed to the Anglican Episcopate, Easter 1988.

Study guide to chapter 9

See general hints on p. 7

Basic

Questions

1. What seems to you most valuable about the Holy Communion service? How could you make more of it?

3. What do you like best and least about your church fellowship? How might you be able to do something positive about your chief dislike, without upsetting other people?

Promise

God's faithfulness – Joshua 1:9; Isaiah 41:10.

Prayers

No. 11 on p. 159 – for our local church.

No. 12 on p. 159 – for a growing appreciation of the Holy Communion.

Extras

Bible study

Luke 22: 7–32

In a group

Each in turn complete the sentence, 'Two of the things I have most appreciated about this group are ...'. How far are those good things true of your whole church fellowship? How could you help some of them to become more true?

Response

Attend a Communion service as soon as possible. If you are a group, share it together.

Check-up

Are you a committed member of a local church, taking part (or preparing to) in their celebrations of Holy Communion?

Suggestions for further reading

David Watson, *I Believe in the Church* (Hodder & Stoughton, 1982). Helpful teaching on both topics by an experienced pastor.

I. Howard Marshall, *Last Supper and Lord's Supper* (Paternoster, 1980). A survey of New Testament teaching and recent debate, with practical suggestions.

10. The Service of Christ

Jesus Christ is presented to us in the New Testament as a servant, indeed as *the* servant, 'the servant of the Lord', the final fulfilment of the servant passages in Isaiah 42–53. He himself said 'the Son of man did not come to be served, but to serve' (Mark 10:45), and again 'I am among you as one who serves' (Luke 22:27). Moreover, we watch him in the Gospels serving God by serving others. He preached, he taught and he healed. He fed the hungry. He washed feet. No service was too menial or too demanding for him to undertake. As Paul put it later, he 'made himself nothing, taking the very nature of a servant' (Philippians 2:7).

Jesus now calls us to follow in his steps, to imitate and even develop the ideals of service which he pioneered. For this is his commission to us: 'As the Father has sent me, I am sending you' (John 20:21; compare 17:18). In this as in everything else he is to be our model. We are to give our lives in service, as he gave his. In the first place, we are *his* servants, as he was the servant of the Lord. Paul, Peter, James and Jude did not hesitate to begin their New Testament letters by designating themselves 'a slave of Jesus Christ'. They knew that he had purchased them, and that in consequence they were his possession and at his disposal. In the second place, their chief way of serving him was to serve other people. 'Though I am free and belong to no man', Paul could write, 'I make myself a slave to everyone' (1 Corinthians 9:19). This means that we are called as Christian people to a double servitude, for we proclaim 'Jesus Christ as Lord, and ourselves as your servants for Jesus' sake' (2 Corinthians 4:5).

Witness and service

But what form will our service take? I want to plead for a much broader, fuller concept of Christian service than is usual among us.

Service' and 'ministry' are both English renderings of the same Greek word *diakonia*. True, especially when the definite article is added, 'ministry' is often thought to be limited to ordained clergy. But Christian ministry is exercised just as much by lay people as by pastors, in secular society as in the church. It is, in fact, an inclusive word for all sorts of service performed by people for people in the name of Christ. First, there are different *forms* of ministry, in response to different needs. Since the neighbour we are to love and serve is a body-soul-in-a-community, we must be concerned for his or her total welfare – physical, spiritual and socio-political. All three can be Christian ministry.

Our priority concern is for people's eternal spiritual welfare, that is, that they may know Christ as their Saviour and Lord. All of us are called to bear witness to him whenever the right opportunity comes. In fact, some writers regard confirmation as (among other things) a commission to witness. But our neighbour's material welfare is also our concern, as we learn from the Parable of the Good Samaritan. The recent debate about the rival merits of evangelism and social responsibility was never necessary. It expressed an unbiblical dualism between body and soul, this world and the next. In any case we are called both to witness and to serve; both are part of our Christian ministry and mission.

Secondly, there are different *kinds* of ministry, determined by the particular gifts and callings of the servants concerned. They can serve by their prayers, their gifts, their interest and study, their encouragement, or their active personal involvement. Thirdly, there are different *spheres* of ministry according to where God has placed us, beginning with our own home and work place, continuing with our local church and local neighbourhood, and culminating in the needs of the wider world. A truly 'holistic' ministry will comprehend these three aspects. Obviously God calls us to specialize according to our particular vocation, gifts, concerns and opportunities. Nevertheless Christian ministry means whole people serving whole people in the whole world.

In this chapter I am going to concentrate on our different spheres of Christian ministry, while not forgetting its different forms and kinds. These spheres are five concentric circles, moving out from our personal 'centre' of home and job through church and neighbourhood to the world.

Christian ministry in our home

According to the Bible marriage is a divine – not a human – institution, and 'God sets the lonely in families' (Psalms 68:6). Indeed, there is a heavy emphasis in Scripture on God's desire for stable, supportive, loving, enriching family life. His ideal is that we begin life in a family, and grow up in relation to our parents and any brothers and sisters we may have, until (according to God's general purpose) we marry and have a family of our own. And at each stage we have a God-given responsibility to all other members of our family. Young people should not treat their home as a hotel, even though of course they should be free to develop interests outside it. Parents should never become so preoccupied with their career or church, their community tasks or leisure occupations, that their children (or spouse) feel themselves demoted to second place. The Book of Proverbs has much to say about parental responsibility for the upbringing of the young.

There is so much in modern western culture which contributes to the disintegration of families (particularly divorce and child abuse) that positive action is needed to keep them united. Christian families, in particular, will refuse to allow television to crowd out family activities, whether outings, sport, music, drama, games or reading aloud. And when members of the family begin to leave home, they will make certain they keep in touch by letters, visits and telephone calls. Then, when all the young people have gone, and the parents are left with each other, and grow old, they know that they will not be forgotten. If one or more members of the family are Christians, while others are not, it goes without saying that they will long to introduce them to Christ – not by preaching sermons, but by their conscientious prayers and consistently unselfish behaviour, while they wait for an opportunity to speak humbly and naturally about Christ.

Christian ministry is wider than this, but it is a true saying that 'charity begins at home'.

Christian ministry in our work

The work place is the second sphere in which we are called to serve, to exercise a Christian ministry. Some Christians understand this in terms of evangelism only. That is, they see their job primarily as pro-

Our daily work is itself a form of Christian ministry.

viding an opportunity for witness to their colleagues or work mates. It is that, especially if they are the only Christian in the business or factory, and especially too if their witness is borne first and foremost by the quality of their work. But our daily work has its own integrity as a form of Christian ministry, quite apart from evangelism. We need a Christian philosophy of work.

The place to begin is Genesis 1, where God represents himself as a thoughtful, creative, diligent and conscientious worker. Having made the world, he continued to supervise, sustain and renew it. Then, when creating human beings in his own image, he made them creative workers also. To remember that in working we are *like God* adds honour and dignity to our labours. Our work gains further importance because it enables us to benefit others, both because by earning our living we are able to support our family and help the needy, and because the product of our work contributes to the common good.

There is, however, an even higher vision of work. God intends us to see it as a stewardship from him, and even a partnership with him, to which he has appointed us. He made the earth, and then told human beings to subdue and rule it (Genesis 1:26–28). He planted a garden, and then put Adam there to cultivate and care for it (Genesis 2:8, 15). Whether the task is global (the earth) or local (the garden of Eden), the same principle of stewardship was in operation. God handed over to human trustees the responsibility to protect the environment and develop its resources. So it is more than a stewardship, in which God is the landlord and we are the bailiffs; it is a genuine partnership in which God has deliberately humbled himself to need our co-operation. He creates; we cultivate. He plants; we develop. What he gives is called 'nature'; what we contribute is called 'culture'. Culture is impossible without nature, since we would have nothing to cultivate if God had not given it. But equally nature has limited value without culture, since God has given us raw materials and left us to convert them into commodities.

Every honourable work, whether manual or mental or both, whether waged or voluntary, however humble or menial, needs to be seen by Christians as some kind of co-operation with God, in which we share with him in the transformation of the world which he has made and committed to our care. This applies alike to industry and commerce, to public services and the professions, and to full-time home-making and motherhood. The great evil of unemployment is that some people are denied this privilege. As for the particular form which our partnership with God will take (i.e., in more mundane terms, what career we will follow, what job we will take), this will depend more than anything else on our temperament and talents, education and training. We should want to be

There are numerous voluntary tasks in every church.

stretched in the service of God, so that everything we are and have is fulfilled, not frustrated.

Christian ministry in our church

When people talk about Christian 'ministry', as likely as not they are thinking about church work, that is, service rendered in the church and for the church, and in particular about the work of clergy. But ministry is not limited to clergy and churches, as we have seen. Nevertheless, our local church is one important sphere of Christian ministry. All Christians should be church members, and all church members should be active in the service of their church.

There are, of course, many voluntary tasks which in every church are performed by a noble band of (often unappreciated) heroes and heroines. I am thinking of good works like cleaning the church, arranging the flowers, making and mending, catering and washing-up, addressing envelopes and licking stamps, showing people to their seats, counting and banking the offerings, keeping the accounts, singing in the choir, playing in the orchestra, reading the lessons, teaching in the Sunday School, leading in the youth club and serving on the Church Council and its committees. These tasks and others are vital for the smooth running of every church.

What is sad is that the vision of lay church work commonly stops there. The reason is that a too rigid distinction is often drawn between clergy and laity, with a secondary distinction between 'pastoral' ministry (which is the clergyman's preserve) and 'practical' service (which lay people may do). Now it is true that in the New Testament the pastor's chief role lies in teaching, which will include preaching to the congregation, counselling individuals and training groups. But there is no reason why these and other 'pastoral' ministries should not be shared by gifted, trained and commissioned lay people. Many Anglican churches have 'Readers'; others are developing a pattern of 'Lay Elders'. Such leaders work in close co-operation with the clergy. They will sometimes preach and lead services, especially the intercessions, assist at Holy Communion, visit, counsel, become Fellowship Group leaders, prepare people for baptism and confirmation, prepare couples for marriage, and supervise different departments of the church's life.

It is a mistake, then, to refer to the pastorate as 'the ministry', because it gives the impression that there is no other. The truth is that there are hundreds of different Christian ministries both in the church and in the community. Mind you, it is a particular privilege to be called into the ordained pastoral ministry. It is 'a noble task' (1 Timothy 3:1), since pastors are 'shepherds of the church of God, which he bought with his own blood' (Acts 20:28). But we should not put clergy on a pedestal. Nor should clergy put themselves there. We should rather recognize the diverse gifts God gives his people, and develop a team of leaders in the local church, clergy and laity, men and women, salaried and voluntary, young and old, whose gifts are used in the building up of the church.

Christian ministry in our neighbourhood

Christians belong to two particular communities, in addition to their home and work, namely their local church (which we have just considered) and their local neighbourhood. Ideally these two geographical areas should largely overlap, and indeed they do if we live in or near the parish to whose church we belong. 'Commuter Christianity' (travelling a long distance to church on Sundays) is understandable in some situations, but it has the serious disadvantage of divorcing our church life from our home and neighbourhood.

All the disciples of Jesus have been 'sent into the world' by him (John 17:18). What then is the 'world' into which he has sent us? And for what purpose has he sent us there? 'The world' does not necessarily mean the planet earth, although we do have a global responsibility and will consider it in the next section. It means rather any part of the human community, far or near, which neither knows nor honours God. In biblical terminology, and specially in the writings of John, 'the world' usually means what we call 'secular society'. Into some segment of it we are commissioned to go. We have no liberty to remain in the security of the church's buildings or in the congenial atmosphere of its fellowship. Of course if our work place is a non-Christian environment, then we already go daily 'into the world'. And the same may be true of our home and family.

Salt and light

But why does Jesus send his followers out into the world? The reason he gave in the Sermon on the Mount is that he wants us to be both its 'salt' and its 'light' (Matthew 5:13–16). Both metaphors indicate that Christians are to permeate non-Christian society, as salt soaks into meat and light shines into darkness. Both imply that he expects us to influence and change society, like salt which inhibits bacterial decay, and like light which reduces and even banishes darkness. Together they illustrate the church's mission. Positively we are to let our light (which is the light of Christ and his gospel) shine, so that through our words and works people come to believe in him. Negatively, we are to maintain so firmly the values and standards of Christ's kingdom that we help to hinder social deterioration.

This includes our immediate neighbourhood. A single unashamedly Christian home can have an enormous influence in the district. And the local church is meant to influence the local community, both by spreading the good news and by involving itself constructively in the life of the locality. We cannot accept the privilege of worshipping in the church and reject the responsibility of witnessing in the parish. It is helpful if each church has its 'Outreach Committee' whose task is to use its ingenuity to devise appropriate ways to bring the good news of Christ to the residents of the parish. It may arrange a house-to-house visitation and/or the distribution throughout the parish of a seasonal message (e.g. at Christmas, Easter or Harvest). It may organize some central events, either in church or in another building, to which all parishioners could be invited. It could ensure that small groups of church members involve themselves in particular aspects of local community life, for example, becoming members of a club or disco, bringing a Christian dimension to one of the social services, or seeing that the public library has an adequate section of Christian books.

All Christian involvement in the local community does not need to be organized by the local church, however. Individual church members will take their own initiatives, partly for recreation, but partly also for service. It is very important for known Christians to serve in local government, to become governors of local schools, and to offer help to one or other of the innumerable services which are needing volunteers, such as the Citizens' Advice Bureau, a drop-in centre for unemployed youth, a hospital or hospice, an old people's home, the local prison or institution for young offenders, a group committed to environmental concerns, or a CARE[1] group concerned to maintain community standards and to provide support and shelter for vulnerable young people.

Christian ministry in our world

It is only in recent years that the growing green movement has popularized the concept of 'one world', namely that the planet earth is like a vulnerable space ship, and that we are responsible for its care and maintenance. Already in the 1960s the distinguished economist Barbara Ward was calling us to develop a sense of 'planetary community and planetary commitment'. Yet we Christians should have pioneered this thinking centuries ago, since the Bible clearly teaches the unity of the planet and of the human race. Every human being is our neighbour, therefore, and their particular race, nation, class or language is irrelevant to our responsibility. It is urgent that, in the name of Christ, we repudiate all narrow parochialisms and develop instead a self-conscious world citizenship. Christian world citizens are committed both to world mission and to world concern.

World mission (sometimes called world evangelization) is not to be dismissed as the hobby of a few fanatics or as incompatible with religious tolerance in our increasingly pluralistic societies. No, it is part of our Christian obedience, for it was the risen Lord himself who issued his great commission, telling us to 'go and make disciples of all nations' (Matthew 28:19). It is a natural expression of God's love, which moved him to give his Son for the world (John 3:16). In addition, God has 'super-exalted' Jesus, giving him the place of supreme honour at his right hand, in order that every knee should bow to him and every tongue confess him Lord (Philippians 2:9–11). If this is God's desire, it must be ours also. Consequently, some are called to become cross-cultural messengers of the good news. 'Missionaries' is their traditional title, although they are often called 'mission partners' today; they share in disseminating the gospel throughout the world. But all of us without exception should contribute in some way to the God-given world mission of the church. The best way is to develop a personal interest in one or two particular missions or missionaries, to inform ourselves by reading about them and corresponding with them, and to support them with our regular prayers and sacrificial giving.

By 'world concern' is meant a parallel commitment to issues of peace, justice and the environment. Because the problems are so many and so varied, we should probably select one or other of them according to our personal and particular interests, and seek to become both informed and involved. Perhaps the best way here is to join a group which is committed to study and action in the area of our concern, whether hunger and homelessness, North-South economic inequality, ecology, the sanctity of human life, racial harmony or human rights.

This brief survey of different spheres of Christian service – home and job, church, community and world – may well appear overwhelming. Each of us has only limited time and limited energy. Indeed, I have found it liberating to recall the simple fact that everybody cannot do everything. Nor should anybody try. For God is building his church, and he calls different members of it to concentrate on different ministries. All of us have a Christian ministry in our home and at our job. These responsibilities we cannot avoid.

But whether we invest the rest of our spare time in our local church or our local community, or in global concerns, or give some time to each, is for each of us to decide conscientiously before God. Our gifts, personality, background, interests and sense of call will help us to discern God's purpose for us. What is plain is that we are called to give our lives in service, and, 'whatever we do', to 'work at it with all our heart, as working for the Lord, not for men' (Colossians 3:23).

> *Teach me, my God and King,*
> *In all things thee to see;*
> *And what I do in anything*
> *To do it as for thee.*
>
> *All may of thee partake;*
> *Nothing can be so mean*
> *Which, with this tincture, 'for thy sake',*
> *Will not grow bright and clean.*
>
> *A servant with this clause*
> *Makes drudgery divine,*
> *Who sweeps a room, as for thy laws,*
> *Makes that and the action fine.*
>
> *This is the famous stone*
> *That turneth all to gold;*
> *For that which God doth touch and own*
> *Cannot for less be told.*

George Herbert (1633)

---

[1] 'Christian Action Research and Education' Trust, 53, Romney Street, London SW1P 3RF

Study guide to chapter 10

See general hints on p. 7

Basic

Questions

1. How would you explain that Christianity is more than just 'going to church on Sundays and saying your prayers' to a non-Christian member of your family who thinks you're becoming a religious maniac?
2. In which of the five spheres of service outlined in this chapter do you think you are weakest? How might you be able to strengthen your contribution in this sphere?
3. What do you understand by the phrase, 'his service is perfect freedom'? How far have you found it to be true?

Promises

Divine wisdom – James 1:5.
God's guidance – Psalms 32:8, 9.

Prayers (Select!)

No 13 on p. 160 – for our daily work.
No 14 on p. 160 – for the service of God.
No 15 on p. 160 – for peace, justice and the environment.
No 16 on p. 160 – for the world mission of the church.

Extras

Bible study

Romans 12:1–13.

In a group

What could you do as a group to complete and cement this course together and at the same time to serve other people? Throw a party for your families or your non-Christian friends? Do a dramatized report on the course for a church meeting? Lead a service together, or do some sponsored activity in a good cause?

Response

Design a 'visiting card' for yourself, listing (in not more than three words each time) your role or function in each of the five spheres of service. Give it to someone else, asking them to pray during the next week for you and all you do.

Check-up

In what ways are you serving Christ?

Suggestions for further reading

Evangelism
Alister McGrath, *Explaining Your Faith Without Losing Your Friends* (IVP, 1989).
A simple account of the Christian faith and how to communicate it to others.
Michael Green, *Evangelism – Now and Then* (IVP, 1979).
Home-making
Lawrence Osborne, *Creative Christianity* (Darton Longman & Todd, 1990).
Edith Schaeffer, *Art of Life* (Kingsway, 1988). Wide-ranging discussions of creative opportunities in domestic and everyday life.
Local church
Michael Griffiths, *Get Your Act Together Cinderella* (IVP, 1989). Key questions about the church today.
Daily work
Leland Ryken, *Work and Leisure in Christian Perspective* (1987; IVP, 1990).
World Mission
John R.W. Stott, *Christian Mission in the Modern World* (American IVP, 1975).
Maurice Sinclair, *Ripening Harvest and Gathering Storm* (Marc et al., 1988).

Conclusion

Your confirmation can be (assuming it is still future) a major milestone in your life, even a turning point to which you will always look back with gratitude. But its significance for you will depend largely on how carefully you have prepared for it.

I greatly hope that, before the day comes when you stand before the bishop and declare publicly that you renounce evil and turn to Christ, you will make sure you have done so privately by opening the door of your heart to him.

I hope too that you will have reflected on the three paragraphs of the Creed so that, when the bishop asks whether you believe and trust in God the Father, in his Son Jesus Christ and in his Holy Spirit, you will be able to respond confidently three times 'I believe and trust in him'.

Then in the years following your confirmation, I hope you will develop disciplined habits of daily Bible reading and prayer, church membership and attendance at Holy Communion, so that, strengthened by these 'means of grace', you will grow in faith, love, holiness and knowledge, obey God's will and commandments, and spend your life in his service, whatever particular forms this may take. Then I believe you will find, as I have done, that the old saying is true: his service is perfect freedom.

Some Prayers

1. For those preparing to be confirmed
Heavenly Father, grant that as I prepare to be confirmed, I may become clear about my relationship to you, so that in the service I may be able to profess my faith with sincerity and boldness, and then receive through the bishop's hands an assurance of your acceptance and blessing, through Jesus Christ our Lord.

2. For the day of Confirmation
I bind unto myself today
 the strong name of the Trinity,
by invocation of the same,
 the Three in One and One in Three.

I bind unto myself today
 the power of God to hold and lead,
his eye to watch, his might to stay,
 his ear to hearken to my need;

The wisdom of my God to teach,
 his hand to guide, his shield to ward,
the word of God to give me speech,
 his heavenly host to be my guard.

Christ be with me, Christ within me,
 Christ behind me, Christ before me,
Christ beside me, Christ to win me,
 Christ to comfort and restore me,

Christ beneath me, Christ above me,
 Christ in quiet, Christ in danger,
Christ in hearts of all that love me,
 Christ in mouth of friend and stranger.
St Patrick's Breastplate, 5th century AD, adapted.

3. For those newly confirmed

Lord, make me an instrument of your peace. Where there is hatred, let me sow love; where there is injury, pardon; where there is doubt, faith; where there is despair, hope; where there is darkness, light; where there is sadness, joy. Divine Master, grant that I may seek not so much to be consoled as to console; to be understood as to understand; to be loved as to love. For in giving we receive, in pardoning we are pardoned, and in dying we are born to eternal life.
Attributed to St Francis of Assisi, died 1226.

4. For those who lack assurance

Lord Jesus, you died for our sins on the cross, and you promise to receive all who come to you, give us grace to rest on your finished work and to trust in your sure word, so that we may know that you have forgiven us, for your name's sake.

5. For perseverance in the Christian life

O Lord God, when you give to your servants to endeavour any great matter, grant us also to know that it is not the beginning, but the continuing of the same, until it be thoroughly finished, which yields the true glory, through him who for the finishing of your work laid down his life, our Redeemer, Jesus Christ.
Sir Francis Drake, 1587, on the day he sailed into Cadiz.

6. For growth in Christian understanding

O Lord, heavenly Father, in whom is the fulness of light and wisdom, enlighten our minds by your Holy Spirit, and give us grace to receive your word with reverence and humility, without which no one can understand your truth, for Christ's sake.
John Calvin, adapted.

7. For growth in holiness

O God, the God of all goodness and grace, you are worthy of a greater love than we can either give or understand; fill our hearts with such love for you, that nothing is too hard for us to do or suffer in obedience to your will; and grant that loving you we may become daily more like you, and finally obtain the crown of life which you have promised to those that love you, through Jesus Christ our Lord.
Nineteenth-century Farnham Hostel Manual, adapted.

8. For a steadfast faith in the Trinity

Almighty and everlasting God, you have revealed yourself as Father, Son and Holy Spirit, and you live in the perfect unity of love; grant that we may always hold firmly and joyfully to this faith, that we may worship your divine majesty, and that we may finally become one in you, who are three persons in one God, world without end.

Church of South India, adapted.

9. For the reading of the Bible

Blessed Lord, who caused all holy Scriptures to be written for our learning: help us so to hear them, to read, mark, learn and inwardly digest them that, through patience, and the comfort of your holy word, we may embrace and for ever hold fast the hope of everlasting life, which you have given us in our Saviour Jesus Christ.

Collect for Advent II, ASB.

10. For help in learning to pray

We ask you, Lord Jesus, as your apostles did, to teach us to pray. For our spirit is willing, even though our flesh is weak. Yet we thank you for permitting us to call your Father our Father. Help us to come to him with the simplicity of a child, to be concerned for his glory and to share with him our needs, for your name's sake.

11. For our local church

Lord Jesus Christ, we praise you that you are building your church throughout the world. We pray for your blessing on the churches of this country, and especially on our own church. May our worship be pleasing to you, our fellowship strong and loving, and our outreach into our parish caring, humble and bold, for the spread of your kingdom and the glory of your name.

12. For a growing appreciation of the Holy Communion

Lord Jesus Christ, we humbly thank you that you chose bread and wine to be the emblems of your body and blood, given on the cross for our sins, and that you commanded us to remember you in this way. Deepen our repentance, strengthen our faith and increase our love for one another, so that, eating and drinking this sacrament of our redemption, we may truly feed on you in our hearts by faith with thanksgiving, for the sake of your great and worthy Name.

13. For our daily work

Heavenly Father, you have blessed our weekday work both by your own work of creation and by your Son's labour at a carpenter's bench: give the nation's leaders the wisdom to solve the problem of unemployment. Enable those of us with work to do, not only to find fulfilment in it ourselves, but also to enjoy the privilege of cooperating with you in the service of the community, through Jesus Christ our Lord

14. For the service of God

Eternal God, you are the light of the minds that know you, the joy of the hearts that love you, and the strength of the wills that serve you: enable us so to know you that we may truly love you, and so to love you that we may fully serve you, for your service is perfect freedom, in Jesus Christ our Lord.
Augustine of Hippo, adapted, died 430 AD.

15. For peace, justice and the environment

Almighty God, you created the planet earth, you make peace, and you love justice. Give your own concern for the environment to those who are destroying it, your peace to the violent places of the world, and your justice to the deprived and the oppressed. And show us what we can do to forward your purposes of love, through Jesus Christ our Lord.

16. For the world mission of the church

Heavenly Father, you have exalted your Son Jesus Christ to the highest place, in order that every knee should bow to him. Thank you that already in every country there are those who confess that he is Lord. Bless those who are seeking to spread his good news. Use the Decade of Evangelism to stimulate others to share in this work. Fill us with your Spirit that we too may bear witness to Christ. And grant that soon the whole world will have heard of him and been given the opportunity to acknowledge him as their Saviour and Master. For the sake of his name.